To Anita
Best Wishes

Grady Hall Morgan

Memoirs of a Greyhound Bus Driver

By Grady H. Morgan

Copyright © 2005 by Grady H. Morgan

ISBN 0-7414-2465-7

Published by:

INFI∞ITY
PUBLISHING.COM

1094 New DeHaven Street, Suite 100
West Conshohocken, PA 19428-2713
Info@buybooksontheweb.com
www.buybooksontheweb.com
Toll-free (877) BUY BOOK
Local Phone (610) 941-9999
Fax (610) 941-9959

Printed in the United States of America

Printed on Recycled Paper

Published March 2005

PREFACE

This is an Anthology of the Author's memories of growing up on a farm in Texas and going to Hawaii when he was eighteen years old. From there he was drafted into the U. S. Navy and he had the tough choice, after the war, of either remaining in Hawaii or coming back home.

After the decision to come home he went to San Antonio, Texas and married the girl he had met while home on leave, two years before.

A year later he and his new bride moved back to California and settled there for good. He held several jobs in sales work but was not happy in any of them. This period was just the beginning of his search for the right job that would bring happiness and contentment, and work that he felt he could excel in. He did not realize, until after his retirement, just how happy he had been in doing what he loved best. Driving a Greyhound bus and meeting people seemed to be what he was destined to do.

From this point the author tries to relive some of the exciting charters he had been on and share with you the places he had been. He also tries to share with you the experience and convenience of taking a trip by bus, while sharing it with a group of your friends.

These are stories he has always wanted to tell and now, after twenty-eight years, he has put some of them together. All the stories in this book are true and told in the author's own words. All pictures used in this book belong to the author or are used with permission as noted. Any errors or omissions are the sole responsibility of the author.

ACKNOWLEDGMENTS

I wish to thank my lovely wife, De, for letting me sit for endless hours at my computer while writing this book. She never complained (though I did receive a lot of kidding) and spent lots of her time watching TV alone, knitting, or sitting and reading books, while I was completely engrossed in the telling of my story.

There were also some trying moments when I told my story of my last days with Linda. It takes a strong person to understand that I had to express my feelings toward Linda in order to tell my story. De has shown those qualities.

I have always wanted to tell the story of my life as a little boy growing up on a farm and having the dream of some day owning and flying my own airplane.

This story is proof that all things are possible. God will help us attain our dreams, if we ask Him to.

All pictures used in this book came from the huge collection of photos shot by the author on the many charters that he truly enjoyed. His picture taking mania has brought many happy moments to him while reviewing the pictures to be used in this book.

Table of Contents

Chapter 1

A DREAM THAT GREW TO REALITY

On April 14, 1924, Dad made a fast trip to town in the old Model T to get the doctor, but when they returned it was too late. I had already arrived in this world.

I grew up on a little farm near Forreston, Texas. We lived quite a distance from our nearest neighbor so I had very few friends during the early part of my life. My dog, Sport, was my closest and truest friend, and I never ventured away from home without him at my side.

My dad bought a twenty-two rifle for me and taught me to hunt at the age of six. A rifle is a dangerous weapon in the hands of most minors, but after Dad showed me what damage the rifle would do, and my nearly shooting my dog, I never forgot about gun safety.

Old Sport and I spent many memorable days hunting rabbits and exploring the countryside. No closer friend and guardian can you have than a dog. I was never drowning, and old Sport never had to jump in and help pull me out, but I know he would have been there, had the occasion ever arisen. He seemed to know and understand when I needed help and he some how communicated with me. I will never forget my dog and the good times we had growing up together. He was like a brother to me. He disappeared one day and I never knew what happened to him. He had been in a fight with another dog and received a severe injury to his head. The injury became infected and old Sport was looking very bad the last few days of his life. I am not sure but I think my dad shot him to put him out of his misery and buried him before I came home from school.

During the Depression I kept my family supplied with fresh rabbits and squirrels. I was also the meat supplier for several families that lived in town.

No one had much money to spend those days but my family was blessed because we lived on a farm. My mother canned several hundred quarts of veggies that we grew in our huge garden each year. We never went hungry at any time because we had chickens, cows, fresh pork and beef when we needed it. We had no money, to speak of, but our need for cash was very small.

I would shell a gunnysack of corn every Saturday morning and we would take it with us when we went into town. We dropped the corn off at the mill and then when we were ready to leave town for home, we would go by the mill and pick up the freshly ground corn meal. The mill kept a portion of the corn for their fee for grinding it, so there was never any money exchanged.

Even during those years my dad could always come up with a quarter for me on Saturday. I would then go to the Strand Theater and spend the afternoon watching a western movie. The movie cost me a dime and a bag of popcorn was only a nickel. After the show I would go off the main street into an alley to Hap's hamburger stand. There I could get the best hamburger I have ever tasted for another nickel, and a soda with my last nickel. That would take care of my quarter and I was ready to go home.

It was at Hap's Hamburger Stand that I learned the difference between a co-cola and an orange crush. When Hap was there I would ask for a hamburger and a co-cola. Hap would cook my hamburger and then ask me what kind of co-cola I wanted. I would say an orange crush or a grape. He knew I didn't want a co-cola. One day Hap was sick and when I came to the stand I told the man I wanted a hamburger and a co-cola. He made my hamburger and then grabbed a bottle of coke and snapped the lid off and set it upon the counter. I stood looking at the coke and the man said, "That will be ten cents." I said, "I didn't want that kind of coke. I wanted an orange coke." The man very patiently explained that coke only made that one drink. If I wanted an orange drink I should have said I wanted an orange drink. I ended up having to drink the coke and it kept coming out my nose and eyes. I could not handle a coke, besides there was only six ounces in a bottle of coke. This little Texan was a fast learner and I have never forgotten since, to say what kind of (co-cola) I wanted.

I was soon in the business of making my own money by selling rabbits to several families in town. I sold them for ten cents a piece or three for a quarter. My business soon grew and it required that I go hunting every day to keep up with the demand for rabbits. There always seemed to be an endless supply of rabbits in my area and always a family to buy them.

I always had change in my pockets from then on so I never had to ask my dad for any more money. I could buy a box of fifty 22 shorts at the Western Auto store for nine cents and I never was one to go around shooting tin cans so my bullets lasted me a long time.

During these times while out hunting or just outside the house, I would hear, on occasion, an airplane flying overhead. This was in the early 1930`s and commercial aviation was just getting started. I would cease doing what ever I was doing at the time and sit down and watch the plane until it was completely out of sight. I would then sit and ponder the miracle of flight. How can anything this large go flying through the sky?

At this time I had never seen a plane on the ground and had no idea of how it could fly through the air. An airplane was so fascinating to watch that I never failed to freeze up when I heard one. I would search the sky until I spotted it and my eyes would be glued to it until it was out of sight. Nothing in my life had ever intrigued me like the thought of an airplane. I grew more excited every time I saw one fly overhead and I knew I had to learn more about them.

My school class was planning a field trip to Dallas, Texas and we were going to visit the Brown Cracker and Candy Company and then go to Love Field. I could hardly sleep at night, because I was so excited knowing I was going to get to see an airplane up close. Time dragged but the big day finally arrived and we were off to Dallas. We were told to bring our lunch and we would eat in some park there in big Dallas. Our first stop was the Brown Cracker and Candy Company. We toured the area where they were baking crackers first. They gave us some fresh crackers just coming out of the oven. Boy, I never tasted anything so good as fresh, hot, salted crackers.

We then toured the Candy Factory. We were told we could eat all the candy we wanted, but do not put any back on the conveyer belt if we did not like it. Who ever heard of a kid not liking candy? That is like opening the gate for a bunch of cattle to enter a garden and saying, do not trample the lettuce. I never ate so much candy in all my life. We were also told not to take any with us, but I think we ate enough while there to last some time.

What a mistake someone made, in planning our visit to the candy factory and then going to the park for lunch! My Mom had made me a super lunch with real store bought bread and stuff, but I was too full of candy to eat any of it.

It could have been the anticipation of my long awaited visit to Love Field that was the cause of my loss of appetite. Then it could have been all the candy that I had just eaten. Whatever the cause, my lunch was not eaten and I thought we were spending way too much time for our lunch break but after an hour delay we finally arrived at the airport.

4

I saw lots of planes sitting out on the field and around large buildings. Later I found out these buildings were called hangers. But how could they hang these planes? They looked too large and heavy to hang.

I sure learned a lot that day about airplanes. I did not see a ramp anywhere out on the field that the planes could use to launch themselves into the air as I believed they did. Boy, was I a dumb little kid. I sure got smart in my knowledge of airplanes and how they worked because I asked many questions and the airplane people did not seem to mind. Maybe they were accustomed to kids asking dumb questions, but I really think they were just happy to be talking about airplanes. I came away from the airport that day with most of the information I had been seeking for months. Now I had a small understanding of how an airplane flew. The most exciting part of this visit to the airport was getting to go aboard a DC-2. It was a twin-engine plane used in commercial flights, and as I remember, it was very plush inside with soft seats and curtains on the windows. It was the forerunner of the most popular and also the workhorse of the Air Force during WWII, The Douglas DC-3.

This was just the beginning of my quest in finding the world of aviation. From that day forward, I knew that someday I was going to be flying one of those planes, and somewhere down below would be a youngster looking up at me and watching in awe, as I winged my way overhead.

There was quite a lapse of time before I really got involved in flying. I was in my teens before I got to take my first flight and by this time, I had read all the material and books I could find on aviation. I understood the theory of flight, what made an airplane move through, and stay in the air.

One day while my family was in town doing their weekly grocery shopping, I noticed a sign advertising an upcoming Air Show. It was to be at some farm two miles north of town. I decided then and there I was going to go see the show the following weekend. My dad said he would drive me out to the field but I would have to get a ride home with someone else, as he would be too busy that afternoon to pick me up.

Back in those years I could hitchhike anywhere faster than you could blink an eye. The first person to come along would pick me up. That does not hold true today nor would I want to be out hitchhiking by myself in this crazy world.

Again the anticipation began building and it was an exceptionally long week. On Sunday morning my dad took me to the area where the show was to be held and we had no trouble spotting the exact place. It was in a huge wheat field, which had already been harvested and was perfect for taking off and landing. There was this huge airplane with big tires sitting near the road. This is where my dad let me out and I walked toward the plane. At that time I was the happiest kid in the state of Texas. I was going to spend the whole day watching this plane fly. As I walked up to the plane I saw a sign reading: "Airplane rides 50 cents."

My dad had given me fifty cents to spend while there but I know he intended for it to be spent on lunch, a hot dog and soda. Oh well, I had gone without eating lunch before.

When we arrived and I got out of the car I saw a Tri-motor Ford sitting in the field. I was so impressed with the Tri-Motor that I completely missed seeing the little Piper Cub sitting on the other side.

In those days fifty cents was a lot of money. It meant a half days work for many people. I was rich. I had fifty cents in my pocket and my dad had given it to me to spend on my lunch.

Well, there goes my lunch money, but I did not care because I am going to take my first airplane ride. I gave the man, sitting at a card table, my fifty cents. He gave me a ticket and said the first flight was full but I could get on the next one. I asked about riding up in the cockpit with the pilot and he told me told that seat was already taken for that flight. I asked about the flight after that and was promised I could get the co-pilot seat then. I waited three flights before I got to board the plane. While waiting, I was admiring the big Tri-Motor taking off and flying over town and then coming back to make the most beautiful landings. It came in and touched down as gracefully as a butterfly lighting on a flower.

A replica of the Tri-Motor Ford

My turn finally came to fly so I go to the cockpit and get in the right seat. The pilot said hi to me and told me to buckle my seatbelt. He started the engine on his side of the plane first, and then started the one on my side. After both were running smoothly, he started the engine on the nose of the plane. He slowly moved the throttles forward and we began to move. There was no wind that day so it did not matter in which direction we took off. Normally, you always take off into the wind but in this case we took off toward town. We slowly gained speed and then we gently left the ground and I was experiencing flight for the first time. We headed for town and I will never forget the breathtaking view of Waxahachie, Texas. I could see everything so clearly and amazingly; such a wide view. I could see the whole town. The old red granite Courthouse stood out majestically and from my view it showed up beautifully. I could see the theater where I spent every Saturday afternoon watching cowboy movies. The people were very small down there and the cars looked like toys. Before I realized what was happening, the pilot had shut down the engine on the nose of the plane and we were headed back to the wheat field. He then explained to me that the center engine was not needed, as we were gliding down for our landing. The big plane seemed to hang in the air so easily and then without feeling it land, we were gently rolling along in the wheat field and we had just finished my first flight.

The pilot was heading to the spot where we had just left only moments before and no turning of the plane was necessary. It seemed I was being cheated or something in that flight. I think I was expecting too much or else it happened so fast my mind could not absorb everything. The memory and the beauty of all I had seen below was too much for my young mind to comprehend in that short time. I was speechless.

My fifty cents was gone and I was going to be hungry before the day was over. Thinking back, I believe it was the smartest investment I ever made. It was a new beginning and a fantastic adventure for me into the field of aviation.

The little Piper Cub was also taking passengers for rides but the price was a whole dollar. Only one person could go at a time and he was just as busy as the big Tri-Motor. Later that afternoon, when passengers were getting hard to come by, one of the fellows in the group put on a parachute and went up in the Cub After the little Cub had struggled and gained enough altitude, the guy in the parachute bailed out. He opened the chute immediately and slowly floated around. I began to wonder if he would ever get down. It was beautiful to watch but it was not something I ever wanted to do and to this day I have never made a jump.

That was the end of the show and now it was time to find a ride home. In those days a person could hitch a ride with no trouble. I got home just about as fast if I had used a car. I was very hungry when I got home and sneaked a bite of something before dinner. For a long time I did not tell my dad I had spent the fifty cents foolishly on an airplane ride because I knew he would not appreciate it, "as much as I did."

I started going to the new airport that had just opened in Waxahachie. Almost every Saturday morning I would hitch a ride out to the airport and there I would spend the day. It was just out of town and I had no trouble hitching a ride so I spent lots of time there. I soon became friends with some of the local pilots and found I could bum free rides by just hanging around. Someone would take me for a ride every time I was out there. We would sometime fly down to where I lived and we would circle the house until someone came outside and I would wave. Some of the pilots would let me fly the plane and I would be on cloud 9. I was in Heaven those days and I still get the same tingling thrill every time my plane breaks the bond of earth and climbs into the air.

Speaking of bumming rides when I was a kid, when I see a boy or girl with their parents watching me as I make touch and goes at my home airport, I never fail to stop my engine and walk over and ask if I can take their kid for a ride. I even take both parents if they want to go. That way I am sharing my love for flying and passing the experience on to another youngster.

I began taking flying lessons in Waco, Texas at the age of seventeen. I only had a few hours logged when I was visiting my favorite aunt and uncle in Temple, Texas. My uncle and I were the greatest of fishing buddies and I spent lots of my time with him. While fishing with my uncle we would talk about my dreams of what I wanted to do when I grew up. It was definitely in the field of aviation. I remember telling my uncle that I was financially unable to pursue my dreams. He suggested I should join the Air Corps at that time and learn to fly and that way I would be paid and I could pursue my dreams to the fullest. I considered what my uncle had said but I was still a senior in high school so would have to put it off for four months.

While my uncle was at work one day I went out to the airport. I happened to be there at the right time when a real cute little plane landed and taxied up to the hanger. No one had ever seen this type of plane before and it caused everyone to be very curious. It turned out to be a completely new type of plane and a large crowd soon gathered. The pilot was from the factory and his purpose of flying around was to introduce the plane to everyone.

This new plane was an Ercoupe. It had twin tails like a P-38 with side by side seating. It was all aluminum and it was stall and spin proof. The demonstrator was out to show off the little plane and was taking everyone who wanted, for a ride. I stood back and never asked for a ride. He probably could tell I was not a prospect for buying the plane. I was just a kid. After he had taken everyone for a demo ride he asked if anyone would like to go to Waco with him the next day. No one spoke up so I stepped up and told him I lived in Waco and I needed to go home tomorrow and would love to fly with him. He said be at the airport at nine the next morning.

I went back to my aunt and uncles house and told them I would be leaving for home a few days early because I was getting an airplane ride back to Waco. They understood immediately as they knew my interest in airplanes and I could always come to visit anytime.

The next morning I was at the airport by eight, beaming with excitement. The Ercoupe pilot arrived shortly before nine and started checking the plane, which had been tied down overnight. He asked if I had ever flown before and I told him I was taking lessons at this time and had two hours logged.

He said, "Good, you can fly us to Waco because I have never been there." When we were ready to leave, he had me climb in on the left side.

This plane has a steering wheel and you drive it like a car while on the ground. I never dreamed he was going to turn the plane over to me completely and let me do all the flying. We taxied out to the active runway and I did the run up. This is a check to make sure both magnetos are working and the controls are operating like they should. After the check, I taxied onto the runway and applied full throttle. We started rolling down the runway.

The little plane was so easy to keep on the centerline it simply amazed me. The Demo pilot pulled the wheel all the way back and told me to hold it there. This was against all principles that I had been learning in my flight training. You do not want to pull back on the controls too hard, as you will stall the airplane. I kept pushing in and he kept pulling back. He won out. He was trying to show me one of the built-in safety features of the plane. By the time we were airborne the nose was at a high angle but we kept moving along and climbing. All the control input that was needed to keep the wings level was to turn the wheel and there was no indication of falling out of the sky. What a marvelous little airplane. It was also spin-proof, which was another safety feature not found on any other aircraft. I enjoyed flying the plane back to Waco and was told before we landed, not to worry about how I brought the airplane down as the landing gear would absorb a thirteen degree impact without bouncing, or hurting the landing gear. Boy, what a sweet little airplane. We were cruising about 105 mph and the trip from Temple to Waco was way too short. Needless to say, I was one happy kid inspired by this little jewel and had a feeling of confidence as a pilot when I taxied up to the ramp and shut down.

At my home airport there were a few guys standing around that knew me and they were probably wondering why I was flying this new plane. Naturally everyone was watching because they had never seen this type of plane before. I was so excited my legs almost buckled when I stepped down from the wing of the Ercoupe.

WW II had not started at this time, and I had just graduated from high school so I decided to join the Air Force. I went to the Army Air Corp recruiting station.

I was turned down because, at that time, I needed two years of college. I immediately went to the Naval Recruiter and was told the same story. I could have gotten into either branch of service as a gunner or something, but I would not settle for any thing less than a fighter or bomber pilot.

England had been at war with Germany for some time now and someone told me that I could go to Canada and join the RCAF with just a high school education and then transfer to the Eagle Squadron so I wrote a letter to Canada. They were accepting American boys for flight training and, yes, I could join the American Eagle Squadron when I finished my training. I would then be sent to Europe.

I decided to go to Canada and was instructed to report to Toronto by a certain date. I was instructed to bring 2 towels, 2 washcloths, 3 pairs of socks, 3 sets of under ware and all essential toilet items. I waited until a couple days before I was to report and departed for Toronto on a Greyhound Bus. When I reached the Canadian border it was easy to spot the young American boys with the same plan I had. It was also easy for the American officials to spot us too. Since the time I had been accepted, the American Authorities could foresee war coming and the need for keeping all their boys at home was essential. We were told if we crossed the border we would be arrested. Needless to say, that ended my dream of becoming a member of the American Eagle Squadron.

I was fresh out of high school and had a job in Waco when I received a letter from an uncle who was living in Honolulu and working as a carpenter in Pearl Harbor. He said he had a good job for me there if I wanted to come over. I filled out the application and returned it. I received an answer immediately and was told to report to an address at the Port of Oakland in California. I immediately packed my clothes and was on my way to Oakland on a Greyhound bus.

When I arrived in Oakland I was taken by bus to the Saint Francis hotel in San Francisco. We were to stay there until we were notified of our departure date for Hawaii. All our meals were taken care of and we were given fifty cents each morning for cigarettes or such. At that time the fifty cents was very much appreciated as I had very little money of my own. Since all my meals were paid for, I could take in a movie every day and still have money left over. We were there a month before our convoy was assembled and ready to sail.

The departure date finally arrived and we were taken to our ship and the convoy finally got underway. It was a traumatic experience for me because this was my first adventure on a ship. We were barely past the Golden Gate Bridge when the sea got rough. The ship began to roll and pitch and I became very uncomfortable. I never lost a meal (I didn't eat very much either) and after a few days the trip was not too bad. I found by going up on the top deck and breathing fresh air I felt good. I stayed up there most all the time from then on.

We finally arrived in Honolulu after eleven days. The convoy only travels as fast as the slowest ship and I just happened to be on the slowest. The USS Henderson, an old WWI cattle boat was put back into service to transport troops. Eleven days on this over crowded, smelly, rolling, pitching, round bottom boat was no fun. There were lots of seasick passengers.

We arrived in Pearl Harbor on March 11, 1942. I will never forget the turmoil and destruction we viewed on arrival. It seemed none of the ships were moved from where they sat during the raid on the morning of December 7th. For the next six months I watched the Oklahoma being rolled over to an upright position and having the water pumped out so it would float. I was working alongside the Sub Base and could watch the submarines come and go. At the time we were building a bombproof telephone exchange to handle all Naval communications in the south pacific.

I fulfilled my contract with CPNAB (Contractors Pacific Naval Bases). I then went to the Honolulu Vocational School to become an aircraft carburetor specialist. After graduation I was sent to Kaneohe Naval Air Station on the windward side of the Island. There I remained until I was drafted and inducted into the US Naval Reserve Inactive. I was told I would remain on my same job. I spent the war years overhauling and flow testing aircraft carburetors at Kaneohe Naval Air Station.

I hitched rides in military aircraft as often as I could. My favorite plane was the PBY-5. It was a twin engine, high wing watercraft, with wheels tucked into the side of the hull to land on either water or runway. It was used for long range searching for the enemy at sea and it could also land in the ocean effectively, to rescue downed pilots. It was very slow and if an enemy was encountered you were in serious trouble. It was dubbed, "The flying Coffin."

There was a group of New Zealand pilots stationed at Kaneohe. New Zealand purchased lots of PV-1 Vega Ventura Aircraft from the USA and the planes were shipped to Hawaii in a dissembled state. On arrival in Hawaii, they were reassembled and flown for twenty hours to make sure all problems were removed before ferrying them down to New Zealand. The Ventura was a twin-engine medium bomber. It was very heavy and fast.

Several times the New Zealanders encountered problems with a carburetor and would bring it in for me to flow test and adjust. I would connect the carburetor to the test stand and run the necessary test. It showed it had been adjusted properly and no need for added correction. They told me the engine would die after takeoff when the throttles were pulled back to cruise power. I would bring the mechanic into the test room and let him see for himself. He would take the carburetor back to the line and install it. After they took the plane out for another flight, he came back to see me with the same results.

After checking the carburetor the third time I decided to go fly with him to see first hand what was happening. That was a big mistake for me. We took off under full power and after leaving the runway behind he pulled the throttles back slowly. This is normal practice with all aircraft but on pulling the throttles back, sure enough, one engine backfired and died. This aircraft was very heavy and not really supposed to fly well on one engine and thank God it kept running. We made it out over the bay and came around to make a successful landing.

These fellows were good friends, but I never flew with them again. They had lots of trouble with the hydraulics in the landing gear and several times had to land with the gear in the up position.

We finally found the problem with the carburetor. The Pratt-Whitney technician had no explanation for the problem but told the New Zealanders to take off and fly for ten hours at full throttle and it would eliminate the problem. Why, we never found out but it did solve our problems

I loved my job and felt I was really involved in the war effort. I was shipping overhauled carburetors to the South Pacific, as they were very much in need for replacements. I did have the advantage of living with my aunt and uncle on weekends since they lived near the base and they were the reason for my being there in the first place.

The war ended and I was discharged but I chose to remain at Kaneohe and work as I had been. My decision did not last long however and I found myself leaving Oahu. My plans had been to remain and live in Hawaii. I had met a gal that I was getting serious with and I had made up my mind to stay there forever. Then all of a sudden I felt I could not stay on the Island another minute. I suppose I had what was called, "rock fever."

When I came home my civilian flying was put on hold. I got married to a girl I had met while home on emergency leave with my mother. Maybe she was part of the reason for my getting rock fever. I will never know. It was not too long before I started a family and could not justify spending money for flying when the money could be put to much better use. There was about twenty-five years with no flying activity during my aviation career. When my children were grown my wife and I got a divorce and for a while I was lost. Nothing seemed to please me. There was a void in my life I could not fill. Then one day a friend told me about an airplane for sale and that rekindled my lost interest in flying and changed my life in general. After looking, I decided to buy the plane, an Ercoupe. I had begun my flying back in 1940 but had given up on it I when I came home and got married.

My first Aircraft, the Ercoupe

Now I was all by myself and I could see no reason why I could not start my flying career again.

I went to the Lodi airport and talked to the instructor about resuming my instructions. I had logged about twelve hours back in 1940 but I had lost my logbook and I had no record of it. The instructor said it did not matter that much, as I would have that much more knowledge about flying and it would not take as many hours. I soloed the Ercoupe in one and a half hours. I flew this little plane for a couple years then decided I wanted something larger and faster.

I went to a Cessna 172, which is a four-place plane but only ten to fifteen miles per hour faster than the Ercoupe. I was satisfied with the 172 for ten years but then I still wanted more speed so I bought a Cessna Centurion. This plane gave me the speed that I was looking for and it was a joy to fly. It had retractable landing gear and it was more comfortable in turbulence than the 172.

About this time I became acquainted with Ed Sprague. Ed was a former big league baseball pitcher. His son, Ed Jr. was attending Stanford. Quite often we would fly my plane over to Stanford to watch his son play baseball. In 1988, Ed and I flew back to Omaha, Neb. for the College World Series Games. Stanford had won the champion ship in 1987 and they were also trying again in 1988. Stanford did win again and we were there to see all the games that week.

At this time Ed Jr. was chosen to play on the Olympic team so Ed Senior and I flew back to Millington, Tennessee for a week to watch the team in their training.

Every night the women of Millington would prepare a beautiful buffet for the team and Ed Senior and I were always welcome to eat with the boys. I got to know each of these players very well and became close friends with several.

The US Olympic team started playing a Chinese team from Taipei (Taiwan) as their final practice. Both teams traveled to Knoxville, Tennessee and put on an exhibition game there. Ed and I followed them in the Centurion. The next day they played an exhibition game in Chattanooga. The game was delayed several times because of rain and finally it ended at one o'clock in the morning. This was a mid-week game and most of the spectators had gone home before the game had finished.

My Cessna 172

The Centurion, my favorite

During the course of the game, the announcer kept saying there was a five hundred dollar gold nugget hidden somewhere on the field and after the game all spectators could come down and look for it. It was buried two inches deep. After the game finally ended there were probably no more than fifty people on the field looking for the nugget. Our team was standing in a group watching the hunt when Ed Senior said, "Grady, go down there and find that thing so we can go home." In the mean time the announcer had narrowed the search to an area between the shortstop and the second base.

I started down onto the field and I remember thinking that it would not be buried near second base, as there would be too much danger of a spike uncovering it during the game. I proceeded to the outfield grass and lined up second base with home plate and then got on my knees and spread my fingers out and started raking the ground for a soft spot. On the second rake I found loose dirt and there was the little white box with the gold nugget. It looked as though I knew exactly where the nugget was hidden. Every time I see one of these players now, after all those years, they still ask if I still have my gold nugget.

The years of associating with the Olympic team are the most memorable time of my life, other than watching all my children grow up.

I will never forget the time when the team came home from Japan, after a week of playing exhibition games over there. This was just prior to the Korea Olympics. I picked them up in the bus used for the Stockton Ports Baseball Team. Ed owned the Stockton Ports team and the bus was idle that day. I was supposed to bring all the players that wanted to come, to Ed`s ranch and lake to spend the fourth of July. When they came out of the S. F. Terminal and were told of the offer, twenty-two of the twenty-five boys chose to come with me.

Ed had told me to call the Pizza parlor, a Round Table he owned in Stockton, while fifty miles away and tell them to start baking the pizzas. They were already aware that I would be arriving with a load of hungry boys. The boys took a large pizza each for themselves and if I remember correctly, I don't think there was any left. They spent a very exciting weekend, swimming and just kicking back

I never watch a baseball game now without seeing one of "my" boys playing. They are all playing for different teams and or have already retired. Life continues for them but their memories I will keep. These fond memories are forever embedded in my memory. Ed Sprague Jr. holds a golf tournament every year and I help with it. The first few years all the Olympic players attended but as they acquired families their responsibilities at home tended to keep them away. There are usually a few however, that still attend each year.

I joined the Civil Air Patrol and was the Deputy Commander for Squadron 72 in Stockton for several years. Being retired, I took advantage of every search going on in California, Oregon and Nevada. I never found any of the downed planes that were the object of the search, but some of the other pilots flying the search found planes to no avail. The pilot and passenger had been killed in the crash.

In these searches we all had maps that had been divided into grids and each pilot flying the search would be assigned a grid and no over lapping grids would be assigned to anyone. This way it eliminates the possibility of two planes flying together at the edge of their grid. I have spent a week at some areas searching for downed aircraft and we remained there until the search was called off. The Air Force reimburses us for all fuel burned during the search and for fuel burned getting to and from the search site. If a search was called and it could be proven there was negligence on the part of the party of the search then the party could be held responsible for the expenses.

I remember on one of my flights down in Texas I had filed a flight plan from San Antonio to Love field, Dallas. I had been calling in and reporting having crossed each waypoint along the way, until I reached the little town of Forreston.

This is the area where I was born and the first time I could view it at this altitude. I decided to turn right and leave my flight plan to see all the places where I had lived when growing up. I was flying at 4500 feet and from that vantage point I could see my birthplace, the second place where we had lived and I could see the grammar school where I started school and the high school where I graduated. All this could be seen from one spot where I was circling. I felt chills run up my spine as I felt I was seeing my whole life unfold down below me.

We then continued on toward Dallas and I was still thinking of what I had seen as I approached. I spotted a large airport on my left that would be even more convenient than going into Love Field. A quick glance at my sectional and I realized the airport was Red Bird. Since I was going to be in need of a rental car I gave Red Bird a call and asked if they had rental cars.

"Yes we do, came their reply." I said we would be right down so we changed our course to Red Bird.

When we landed and taxied up to the office I was told by an employee to leave the plane where it was sitting and he would take care of it later. We went inside the office and took care of the car rental and one of his employees took the car to the plane and proceeded to put our luggage into the car. He asked how long we would be staying with them and I said a week. He said there was supposed to be a big storm coming in that night but not to worry about the plane because they would take care of it.

We got into the car and drove to a nice motel nearby that he had recommended and got checked into our room. We were both hungry and we had seen a nice place near the motel serving seafood so we went there. We had just been seated when I said,

"Oh my God!"

I jumped up and my wife said, "What is the matter?"

I said, "I forgot to close my flight plan!"

I ran to a telephone and called flight service and told the man I needed to close my flight plan and gave him my N number on the plane.

There was a hesitation and then he said, "Mr. Morgan, you are a very lucky man. We traced you from San Antonio to Waco and there we lost track of you. We have contacted all airports in between and we checked with Love Field, your final destination. No one had a record of you landing so we presumed the worse had happened. I was just calling to activate a search but the line was busy." "You do realize this could have been a costly experience for you had the search been activated, don't you?"

I did not even try to explain the reason for forgetting to close my flight plan as this man had already given me verbal beating that would live with me forever.

All I could say, "I am sorry and it will not happen again."

With that settled, I went back and joined my wife at our table and we had a very delicious seafood dinner.

That is the last time I ever filed a flight plan on any of my trips. Do not get me wrong, you should file a flight plan or call and get flight following for your trip. I prefer flight following over filing a flight plan simply because something might happen while in flight and all you have to do is press the mike button and say, "May Day." The Air Traffic Controller knows exactly where you are and can usually summon help to your location before you get to the ground.

I know from personal experience that a flight plan does not even begin to take effect until you have been over due for an hour. Then there is the time spent checking all the airports along your route to see if you have made an emergency landing somewhere. The Air Force is then notified and the search gets put into motion. This process takes time as the CAP squadrons in the area of the missing plane have to call in their pilots and in the meantime you could be bleeding to death.

Most pilots dislike talking to anyone connected with the Federal Aviation Administration. They are afraid the FAA will find something wrong with them or their plane. Out of sight out of mind so to speak. They are wrong in that respect because all the people that work in the Air Traffic Control rooms are people like you and me. Some are pilots and are there to help you in case of need and will treat you with the utmost respect. Try throwing your weight around and playing the big shot and you will wind up in a holding pattern. I have spoken with lots of ATC people and they are human and will treat you as nice as you treat them. Sure they wear the big gun and can apply pressure where it is needed. Possibly that is the reason most pilots do not like to talk to ATC any more than necessary. However, it just gives me a good feeling to know they can have help waiting for me should the need ever arise.

I left the Civil Air Patrol to fly for the San Joaquin County Sheriff's Department in 1990. The Department owns a Cessna 206 that I am qualified to fly. I prefer using my Cessna 150 when I am looking in the cornfields for marijuana. I can fly at a much slower speed and the 150 makes a good search platform.

One day I was checking to see when my medical was due (good for two years) and since it would be due in three weeks, I decided to go get it renewed. I am Diabetic but keep my blood sugar controlled by medication. I had not been checking my blood sugar for the past week and when I took the medical I flunked the test because it was too high. In three months, if I got it back down in the acceptable range, I could get my medical back. It hurt me deeply to loose my right to fly but I figured I had been gifted to be able to fly as long as I did. After giving my situation a lot of thought I decided not to renew my medical and gave up flying.

I put my plane out by the frontage road at the Lodi Airport and had for sale signs in the windshield and windows with the price and my name and phone number on them. I then got in my car and drove home. On arrival at my house, the phone was ringing. When I answered it there was a fellow wanting to see me for more information about the plane. I told him I would be right there and drove back to the airport. I talked to the man for fifteen or twenty minutes about getting a hanger and so forth and I told him I would see to it that he could keep the same hanger that I had. With that, he pulled out his checkbook and wrote me a check for the full asking price.

That was in the summer of 2002 and I have never flown another plane since. I am still a member of the Sheriff's Squadron but without a plane. There is a need for observers and I can fill that duty.

Everyone said I was making a big mistake in selling my plane but honestly, I have no desire to fly any more. I feel God has been good to me and in all my flying He has let me enjoy life without ever having a single accident. I have had a few exciting times while flying but always learned from my experience.

There comes a time in life when we must give up a few of our pleasures and I felt the time had come for me to clip my wing. I had many happy hours of flying during my lifetime and I thought this might just be the time to stop.

You have to stop sometime.

Chapter 2

MAKING THE RIGHT DECISION IN LIFE

After I had been discharged from the Navy, and had returned to the states, I went to Yuba City, California to visit my Mother. I had mixed feelings as to what I wanted to do with myself. I had met this beautiful girl, Juanita, in 1943 while I was home on medical leave, during my mother's surgery. Juanita's father was a Lt. Colonel at Beale Air Force base, a few miles out of Marysville, Ca.

The war had ended now and she had gone back to San Antonio with her family. Her father had been transferred back to Ft. Sam Houston.

I was having a problem now, trying to decide what I should do. During the last couple of years I had been corresponding with Juanita, and I had fallen in love with her or I thought I had. Now I had a decision to make, go back to Hawaii and live or go down to San Antonio.

I had been discharged in Honolulu with the intentions of getting married to an Island girl and staying in Hawaii. The Islands were paradise to me and I think I left a large part of myself there when I moved away. I wanted to make my home there and stay forever, although my feelings for San Antonio were also having a huge effect on me because I had fallen in love with Juanita.

San Antonio finally won the battle and I found myself saying goodbye to my mother and heading to San Antonio. Hawaii would have to be put on hold.

I arrived in San Antonio and was greeted by a very happy little Texas gal. She was very glad to see me as it had been over a year since we had seen each other. About six months later we were married in the Lakewood First Christian Church. My wife worked for the telephone company at that time and I had started working for the San Antonio Rapid Transit as the Station Foreman. We were happy with our jobs but we both had a yearning to return to California. After much thought, we packed our belongings, which were not much at that time, and moved to Paradise, California.

Two of my uncles lived there and we both liked the little mountain town. I bought a lumber truck and got a contract hauling for a lumber mill there in Paradise. I did this until the lumber mill had to close because of new environmental laws so I was looking for another source of income.

A friend, who had a freight business operating from Chico to Paradise, had used my truck and me several times when business was heavy. He asked me if I would drive for him if he started a bus line from Chico-Paradise-Sterling City. I accepted the job and drove the bus for a while. Not seeing a future in that job I left and got into route sales work and we moved down to Yuba City.

There I went to work as a cake and cookie salesman for Hostess Cake. A year later I was transferred to Stockton, California and became a Wonder Bread salesman. Wonder Bread and Hostess are both owned by the Continental Baking Company. I enjoyed my job as a bread salesman, but having just opened the Stockton area market with Wonder Bread, the pressure for higher volumes of sales was tremendous for all the salesmen. A bread route is an entirely different business than most selling jobs. You have to sell every loaf every day. If you do sell it all you would think you had done a good job. No way, your supervisor says you did not have enough bread out there.

Now, have a real bad day and pick up a lot of stale bread and you had too much out there. It is a no win situation. It does not matter that your competition is experiencing the same good and bad days as you because it will still be your fault. Ten years of that and after a heated discussion, I threw my route book down on the supervisor's desk and told him to operate the route as he saw fit. That was the day my route sales work ended.

During this time I had become a father to three children, two girls and a boy. I had responsibilities now and I wanted a job that paid above average wages and one that I could look forward to going to each day. I was also looking for a job that had a good retirement plan. With Wonder Bread I had the good wages and would have had a good retirement but I simply could not stand the daily pressure. I was at the age where I had to make a decision very soon. I had already put my application in with Greyhound and was waiting until the Drivers Training Program started. I had also put in an application with the California Highway Patrol but the waiting list went on forever.

I was sure now of my decision to go with Greyhound. I took a nice vacation with my family and was ready to have a fresh start with Greyhound when the training program started three weeks later.

The training program would take six weeks to make us bus drivers. We had class work one day and we would go out driving the next day. The classroom work consisted of learning to handle tickets and making out our daily reports. We also learned how to keep a daily log of our time while we were on and off duty, driving or not, everything had to be logged for the twenty-four period each day.

At the start of our schooling, there were 34 student drivers. The first day we were given a questionnaire to fill out concerning our driving record. Any and all traffic violations that we had acquired through out our life were to be listed, whether we thought they were of any significance or not.

We were told we were wasting their time and ours by not reporting all violations. Some of the fellows figured the little fender bender they caused down in Biloxi, Mississippi would go unnoticed here in California. We soon found they were not kidding about not reporting accidents. Each day there would be one or two missing from class. When we would ask what happened to them, we were told they had had an accident ten or twelve years ago in some other state that they had not reported.

All of our names had been given to an Agency that does nothing but track down a persons driving record. Little did I realize just how important my driving record would become later in life.

Not only should it be a clean record, but it better be kept that way while driving Greyhound buses. If you had three accidents in your personal car, you have ended your driving career with Greyhound. You may think that is being too harsh on someone but we were transporting human beings, not hay or cattle.

Greyhound also taught us that accidents do not just "happen," they are created by not paying attention to the situation before and around you. The car that you thought appeared from out of the blue was there all the time and you did not see it.

The more I drove and the more safety classes I attended, the more I had to agree with them. Barring mechanical problems, there is no reason for any accident. I have only been in one accident in my life and I had nothing to do with it except my being an innocent passenger but that one was definitely preventable.

I had reached the age of sixteen and I joined the CMTC (Citizens Military Training Camp) for a month during the summer of 1939. I hitchhiked down to San Antonio and reported to the military base at Ft. Sam Houston. We boarded trucks in a convoy to be transported out to Camp

Bullis, twenty miles northwest of San Antonio. The truck I was in was actually a large pickup type with two boards across the back and three boys sat on each of the boards. I rode in the front seat with the driver. The windshield was folded forward toward the engine.

On the way out to camp, the truck we were in, tried passing a supply truck and trailer going down hill. Our truck had a governor on it and when it reached top speed it would go no faster. The supply truck and trailer naturally gained speed going down hill. We were not moving any faster than the supply truck when we came upon a blind curve at the same time.

Whoops! There comes a car. Our driver put on the brakes to slow down and tried to get back behind the supply truck and in doing so, he overturned our truck, scattering the seven boys along the rocky roadside. My Guardian Angel was riding with me that day because I was thrown between two large rocks that could have broken my back or killed me, had I hit either of them. When I came to I found myself wedged between the rocks, I slowly started moving each part of my body to see if anything was broken and after feeling no broken bones I closed my eyes and thanked God for my good fortune. The next thing I remembered was hearing voices from two fellows standing over me, and one saying, "This one looks like he is dead."

I was very much alive and I told them so. I was then loaded into one of the ambulances that traveled with the convoy and taken back to Ft. Sam Houston to the hospital. There I spent a week before being released to go home. I never did get out to Camp Bullis.

One of the boys sitting in the rear of the truck was killed. The driver had to have his left arm amputated and all the other boys had arms, legs, ribs and collarbones broken. I was the only one out of eight people aboard the truck that had no serious injuries. My injuries consisted of one small cut on my side along with many small thorns in my back from my encounter with a brier patch after I exited the truck.

Conclusion: This accident was definitely avoidable.

We should never have tried passing this truck while going downhill when at the bottom a blind curve was in sight. Since we were only one mile from the camp there was no need to hurry.

Getting back to my new career. I said before, we spent a day driving and the next day having class work. On the days that we drove, there would be five trainees on each bus. One trainee would drive the bus from the San Francisco depot and we would go to Fresno, our southern most division point. We would pull through all the Greyhound depots on the way and there would be driver changes quite often. All five of the trainees would do lots of driving and at the same time we were learning where all the depots were and how to enter them. We took notes on how to find some of the depots.

The next day would be spent driving to Redding, which was the end of our division to the north. Reno, our eastern division point would be on the next days driving agenda. It was enjoyable because we had the same instructor and we were with the same student drivers so we got to know each other better. We could stop along the way any time we wanted to get a soda or just to get out and stretch.

We had been at this for about a month and beginning to feel we were becoming old timers at handling the buses. We took a different model bus each day so we would be familiar with all the buses in our fleet.

Now that we were comfortable with operating the buses and knew how to handle all the paper work, we were given an itinerary so that we would actually operate a regular schedule under supervision, with real passengers.

Fourteen drivers out of the original thirty-four that started now remained in the program. That tells you that Greyhound is very strict in choosing the drivers they hire. If the driver did not meet their qualifications, he was not hired. Today it is a different story. They have to hire anyone that comes along, regardless of qualifications.

It is game time now and we no longer will be driving around having fun. We are to pickup the tickets and operate the schedule as if we were the regular driver. The regular driver stands back behind us and is there to help, only if we have a question or any type of problem. At this time, we are supposed to be capable of doing the job completely with no help.

I pick up the tickets and load the passengers, and then I make sure the baggage doors are closed tightly. The regular driver stands back out of the way pretending not to be watching. He has the right front seat reserved and for this trip he is just another passenger, getting paid but not having to work.

The first trip out of the depot and across the San Francisco Bay Bridge, needless to say, strained my nervous system completely. By the time I got through with the mad rush of entering and reloading at the Oakland depot and getting back to the freeway, I felt the worst that could happen was over and I had decided I was going to be a real Greyhound Bus Driver after all.

I am on my own now and if I should have an accident, it will be my responsibility. By this time I have had enough experience driving and the instructors have already cleared me as being competent to handle the bus so I am on my own. We have already gone through a reaction test to see how fast we recognize an emergency and to see how quickly we can get on the brakes. We have already proven ourselves as drivers.

I held the record in my division of thirty eight hundredths of a second for recognizing danger and reacting by apply the brakes in that amount of time.

Just getting into and out of some of our depots proved beyond any doubt that we could handle the bus with no problem. Sacramento is a good example of a tight squeeze. You had to make a left turn from a one-way street, into an alley. On the left of the entrance to the alley, were three large steel posts, protecting a fireplug. Apparently it had been hit too many times before. On the right side of the alley was the brick wall of the Woolworth store. You cannot move over in to the right lane to give more clearance in starting your turn, so every move has to be calculated just right.

After the ten days of operating all the schedules with a regular driver, we were now ready to bid a position in the system and become an everyday part of it. From that day forward we were on our own.

We are Greyhound Bus Drivers!

***

Every six months, every run and extra board position in the system is open for bid. The man with the most seniority naturally gets his choice first and then on down the line to the newest of drivers. The new driver gets what no one else wants and has to take the worst runs. That was the reason I chose to work the extra board out of Stockton, because I, as a new driver, could not hold a decent run.

There were usually about thirty drivers on the extra board in Stockton. The way the board works is quite unique. When you come in from work your name is placed on the bottom of the list of drivers. When the next service is needed, which may be a run to cover, an over load of a regular schedule, or a charter. The man on top of the list gets the job. When your name works to the top of the board you are assigned the next service. Sometimes it gets up there too fast. We had to have eight hours between each tour of duty and when we were at peak season it was just that, eight hours.

I preferred working the extra board, as I would be doing something different every day. We had seven regular schedules a day out of Stockton going to Lake Tahoe. This was a choice run to have but it required high seniority to hold. By working the extra board you would get the overloads and it paid the same as being on the regular run. We also had lots of charters that were worked from the extra board and they were always interesting. We went on lots of trips to baseball and football games and the drivers always got to go to the game free.

When we would stop for lunch or dinner with a group, the driver usually got a complementary meal or word would spread fast among the drivers and no one would stop there again. We soon knew all the restaurants that would comp us from all over the central valley. We always stopped at these restaurants at meal times to give them our business and get a free meal.

I drove charters for several groups that must have thought I treated them above average, because they would always request me for their next trip. Lots of the drivers would get out of the bus, light up a cigarette and let the passengers get off the bus by themselves. I never did that because first of all it was part of my job to see that each passenger got off the bus safely. I made a habit of taking each person by the arm as they were coming down the steps to help them if they should stumble. The Lodi Travel Club was one of the groups I drove for regularly. I made them feel at home on my bus and would be more than happy to stop anytime they wanted. It paid off by getting me lots of request charters.

The group had to write a letter requesting a certain driver if they wanted him to drive their charter. That driver would then be notified of his upcoming charter. He could accept or refuse it if he wanted.

While driving for Greyhound, I took many enjoyable trips while covering all the eleven Western States. I got to see all the National Parks in the Western US and most of Western Canada. This was a dream come true.

It was an extremely tough job though, but someone had to do it.

Chapter 3

A TRIP TO THE ASTRODOME

I recall a trip to Houston, Texas, and while we were going across the desert out of Mojave, someone asked me if I knew the name of a beautiful flower that kept popping up in the desert. We kept seeing them as we drove along the high way just out of Mojave. I told them it was brought into this country from the Amazon River and how fortunate we were to get to see it blooming.

"What do I know about flowers, I am just the bus driver," I said.

At the first opportunity to safely leave the road, I would pull the bus off the road and into the desert where the flowers were blooming and we got out for a closer look. Try that today with the environmentalists and I would be spending time in prison.

It was little things like this that made the trips enjoyable for everyone. First of all they could not visualize a Greyhound bus off the roadway. A lot of the passengers were not able to walk too far, so I could put them up close to Mother Nature. It also made them feel the bus was their private car. Even if they were in their car, I doubt anyone would have driven out into the desert like I did with the bus. This was one of many ways that we enjoyed the trips and had something to remember afterwards.

I thought nothing of stopping the bus to get out and pick up a pretty rock for someone to take home for a souvenir.

We were east of Albuquerque on I-40, on that same trip and had just turned south headed for Roswell, New Mexico, when all of a sudden we heard an ear splitting high pitched, shrill noise coming from the rear of the bus. I immediately pulled off the road and went back to see what had happened. To the best of my mechanical knowledge I determined it to be the generator. I could not take the belt off the generator to stop it from turning, as it would make the engine run hot, plus the air conditioner would not work. I definitely would need another bus brought to me at Roswell, since we would be spending the night there.

I called El Paso, as that was the closest place to Roswell that would have buses, and told the dispatcher I would be needing another bus before leaving Roswell the next morning. He told me, when I got into Roswell, to take the bus to the New Mexico Stage Lines shop as they were authorized to work on our buses. The trip on to Roswell was a nightmare. We had no alternative but to contend with this ungodly high pitched screaming of the generator. I tried driving at different speeds but to no avail, the noise was ear piercing. I finally had the rear seat passengers move up and sit on the armrest of seats in front of the bus. Some spread coats on the steps and four ended up sitting on the steps.

We finally arrived in Roswell and I can truthfully say this was the most unbearable time and the worst nightmare I have ever encountered on any trip or at any time during my career as a bus driver.

After getting everyone settled in our motel I took the bus over to the New Mexico Stage Line. The mechanic agreed it was the generator but said he had no generator or parts that would fit my engine. It was too late now to have one sent from El Paso without holding us up the next morning. This was always one of my worst fears while driving a charter. You had your motels all arranged and being late one day would create havoc with reservations for the rest of the trip.

A shear pin had broken inside the generator and the mechanic said his only choice was to weld the pulley to the shaft and if he did that it could never be fixed when I did get to a Greyhound shop.

I said go ahead and weld it, so he did. When I drove back to the motel it was so quiet in the bus I almost went to sleep. Anyway, that problem was solved forever. We had no more trouble and when we returned to Stockton the bus was sent into San Francisco and it probably lasted until they retired the bus.

The next morning was a real treat, a beautiful day and a quiet bus. We continued our trip south. We were headed for San Antonio but we made a left turn for Fredericksburg, Texas where I met my Daughter, Sylvia, and had lunch with her on the way to the LBJ Ranch. Mr. Johnson was president at the time and he just happened to be home so we could not get close to his place. We did get to the gate of his property and that was as far as we could go. Apparently, my being a fellow Texan did not carry any weight with the guard at the gate.

The trip from Fredericksburg, all the way to Blanco, provided us with the most spectacular scenery of Blue Bonnets and Indian Blankets. We were going through uncultivated fields and pastures that were blanketed with flowers. This was an added attraction. After lots of picture taking, we continued our journey to San Antonio.

We checked into a hotel near the Alamo. The San Antonio River ran right behind the hotel and by exiting the rear door we found ourselves on the river. The pathway along the river was spectacular at night. The trees were covered with small blinking white lights and it was so beautiful just strolling along the pathway. There are many restaurants all along both sides of the river that serve delicious authentic Mexican food. You can go aboard one of the little boats that go back and forth along the river for a view of the entire length of the river and all the lights. San Antonio is a beautiful city with

Mexican accents through out. We spent a restful two days there before moving on to Houston.

My daughter Sylvia, and me

***

It is ironic that I was born in Texas but I had never been to Houston. I was married in San Antonio and I had traveled most of Texas while I was living there. I had even gone to Corpus Christi for a job I had with the Naval Air Station after the war, before I was married. It was cold and damp and I was lonely being down there all by myself, so I went back to San Antonio and never took the job in Corpus Christi.

Now after all these years I was driving a Greyhound Bus to Houston for my first visit. The main purpose of this trip was to see the Astrodome and visit The Carlsbad Caverns on the way home. As we came into Houston I decided I should stop and get directions to our hotel, since I had not done my homework the night before.

I had noticed a temperature sign along the street while coming into town that read 78 degrees. I welcomed this because it was very hot with high humidity in San Antonio. I pulled to the curb by a Texaco Station and walked over to the attendant, fueling a car. I immediately felt my shirt clinging to me with dampness, as the humidity was 95 percent out there on the street. I asked the attendant if he could tell me how to get to our hotel and he carefully laid the pump down along side the car, and putting his hand on my shoulder, he walked back to the sidewalk with me and pointed the way. I felt sorry for the poor lady sitting in the car waiting for her tank to be filled, but she gave me a big smile of approval and did not seem to mind. I found that people in the south would go overboard to assist you in any way.

We were there to see a four game series between the Houston Astros and the San Francisco Giants. Seeing the Dome the next day, I thought, there is no way you could play baseball in there. When we entered the stadium and started down to our seats, the farther we went, the higher the ceiling seemed to be. During the games there were some balls hit very high but they never came close to the ceiling. The playing field must have been over a hundred feet below the surface of the outside ground level.

One day we drove to Galveston, Texas to see the Island and have dinner. Galveston is located on the southern coast of Texas. We took a tour of the city on one of the little tour trams and we were told how the city had been destroyed during one of the big hurricanes. The Island is only a few feet above sea level and it floods easily during any significant storm. It was an enjoyable trip down and we took a side trip on the way back to see the USS Houston, a WWII battleship, now berthed in the river, just out of Houston. We had to take the bus aboard a small ferry to cross this same river in order to get back to Houston.

I do not think I could ever grow to like the oil smell of Houston nor could I tolerate the humidity there. We toured the city and saw many beautiful homes, most of which were priced so far out of reach to the average citizen that it is not realistic to even think of owning one. I assume the oil smell that I found to be very offensive is actually the smell of money. Maybe I could grow to love it with a few oil wells of my own. One of my dislikes of Houston was the humidity. The temperature was not all that bad but combined with the humidity it was more than I could be comfortable with.

It was time to start our trip back home but we wanted to go through Dallas and see the place where President Kennedy was shot. We were to be there three days and I was looking forward to getting to visit my Dad while we were there. He lived in Ft. Worth and I had just gone back the summer before to visit him. I gave him a call to see if he would be home and told him I was there on a business trip and would like to come over and spend the night. He had nothing planned so I drove over to his house. He was certainly surprised when he heard the bus in front of his house.

When we were on charters sometimes, we would use the bus as we would our car. There was never anything said about using it (I never told the company I did this). The only time I would have gotten into trouble was if I had had an accident while "off route" so to speak. I had a nice visit with my Dad and after breakfast the next morning, I deadheaded the bus back to Dallas to pick up my group and begin our journey home.

My Dad and Me

Our next stop was the Carlsbad Caverns. If you have never been to the Carlsbad Caverns you should make plans to go there. You cannot imagine the spaciousness of some of the rooms down in the Cavern. You are almost a thousand feet below sea level when you reach the bottom. You can walk down, which I would advise if you feel capable of walking a short distance. Most of my group did walk all the way down. The first part of the trail is a little steep but there are rails to hold onto and places to sit and rest. You will see the place where millions of bats are sleeping, whereas you would miss this if you took the elevator.

After the first part of the trail where the bats are, it levels out somewhat and the going is not too bad. I have been in the Caverns several times and I have always walked down along with most of my group.

Once you are down to the bottom, the trails get a bit wider and it is smooth asphalt, so the walking is easy. There are lots of benches and places to sit and enjoy the view. You see beautifully formed stalagmites (reaching for the ceiling) and stalactites (hanging from the ceiling). It takes the better part of the day to view this phenomenon. You can also have lunch at the foot of the elevators and then ride one to the surface. That is about all there is to see in this area but it is well worth the trip.

I purchased a Golden Age Passport card, years ago for six dollars and it gives me, and all my party, free entry into any of the National Park in the United States. I would highly advise purchasing it if you do not already have one. The cost is just ten dollars now and you will save that price on the very first park you visit.

We drove back to our motel and prepared for the beginning of the long trip back home. This trip was fifteen days total and the group was eager to get home and start planning for the next one.

Many of the groups that I took on charters provided a room for me so they would have the bus handy should they need it. The Lodi Travel Club did not provided me with a room and I had to find my own each day after we arrived at our destination. Most of the drivers in Stockton thought the Lodi Club was known for not tipping generously but I did enjoyed being with them. The places they stayed were usually too expensive for my budget so I had to look else where for my room. I still loved to be with them and had to overlook their faults.

They always gave me four dollars per day for my tip on the trips. All other groups would usually give you a minimum of twenty dollars per day plus have your room reserved and paid for. They wanted their driver to keep the bus with them and not have to go out looking for a room.

I remember on almost every trip the tour conductor for the Lodi Travel Club would always tell everyone on the bus to leave a nice tip after his or her meals.

My tip was always given to me at the start of each trip in an envelope and the tour conductor made sure everyone saw her giving it to me. No one ever knew how much was in the envelope and I never complained.

***

The Lodi Travel Club had gone to Houston in April, and the next trip had already been planned for a visit to the Grand Canyon and then through the Canyon lands of Utah.

This trip was for fifteen days and we headed south through Bakersfield, Mojave, Needles and Kingman. From Kingman we drove north to the Grand Canyon. The group stayed in the El Tovar Hotel, which is a beautiful old stone building that was once a Harvey House.

The train came up from Williams each day and stopped directly across the street from the Lodge. The Lodge was built in 1905 for the Santa Fe Railroad. The Santa Fe Railroad built large hotels, about one days travel along the railroad, and used them for meals and overnight accommodations in the early days of rail travel before the Pullman coaches became an addition to trains. These hotels were called Harvey Houses. There is one located in Winslow, Arizona. This hotel has been closed for sometime but is now opened again to the public. I visited this one just a short time ago and they have started a complete remodeling project on the hotel and when I was there it was half complete. It is located by the Santa Fe tracks and was convenient for the passengers to leave the train and have lunch or dinner. The yard is beautifully landscaped and it will be a monumental showpiece, when finished.

A view of the Grand Canyon

The Grand Canyon is a good place to go and relax and enjoy the scenery. If you are on the plus side of fifty you will not want to be taking any hikes down into the canyon. If you are young and into hiking, and with a little more ambition, then hiking a trail down to the bottom of the canyon would be your thing. Me, I am just happy to look over the rim of the canyon and take pictures.

My group only stayed two nights there, as that was sufficient time to take in all the observation points along the south rim. The second morning we left to go around to the north side of the Grand Canyon to start our journey thru the beautiful Canyon Lands in Utah.

As we left the Grand Canyon to the east, we went down hill for quite away. When we intercepted highway 89, I made a right turn and drove about a half mile or so and there I turned off to my left and pulled into an observation area for the

Little Colorado River. If you have never looked down into the Little Colorado you are in for a treat. The walls of the river are made up of huge rocks. I mean UPS truck size.

View of the Little Colorado

They are huge and are stacked one on top of each other in such a neat stack that you would think it was done by man. The river is a long ways down too. It gave me chills to look over the side. When I first visited this area years ago, there were no railings to keep you from falling over. I got down on my hands and knees to worm my way close enough to see over the edge. Now there are railings installed, I suspect, because a few people had fallen over the edge.

We continued our journey to the southwest corner of Colorado to visit the cliff dwellers of Mesa Verde. It was a long climb up the mountain to reach Mesa Verde but well worth it. This is an area where the cliff dwellers built their homes in the cliffs many years ago. There would be a whole community of the dwellers in twenty or thirty rooms, grouped together. All of a sudden, for some unknown reason, they all pulled out and abandoned their villages. No one knows when or why the cliff dwellers left. Possibly a drought or plague struck the village causing them to look for greener pastures elsewhere. It was interesting looking at the remains of their homes and wondering where they had gone and why they had left. We got lots of pictures.

From Mesa Verde we went to Moab, Utah and spent the night there. The next morning we left Moab and a few miles out of town we entered the Arches National Park. The entrance of this park takes you up the side of a mountain that has the most beautiful large red sandstone boulders and spires. It will keep you on the edge of your seat. Once you get leveled out and start through this valley you will start seeing arches of this colorful, magnificent red material. There will be tower like columns standing alone with nothing near them for miles. It is a spectacular sight to see. You marvel at Mother Nature and think of all the years it took to create these spectacular monuments.

We left the Arches National Park and entered the Canyon Lands National Park, which was located only a few miles down the road. We parked the bus at the Visitors Center and loaded into several little yellow jeeps. The jeeps took us out onto the rocks and into areas no cars could possibly go. It was an interesting trip and we were taken to an arch that was probably 150 feet across and we could walk over it. Most of the group chose not to try. We went to the edge of Dead Horse Canyon to look down at the river hundreds of feet below. The story goes that a herd of wild horses were marooned on the plateau on the rocks above the river. They could smell the water below and became so thirsty they jumped over the edge.

True? Might be.

After the Canyon Lands we went to Capital Reef National Park. This Park is beautiful and, by all means, if you are in the area you should see it. There were many beautiful rock formations and the road followed a small stream thru the mountains, which had very beautiful scenes for picture taking. We saw lots of wild life feeding along the little stream while we were there. This was not my favorite spot on the tour, but still worth seeing if you are in the area. We took a dead end road that went to the southern end of the park and had to return by the same route. Around every turn there were rock formations that would leave you in awe and some rocks with such odd shapes it made you wonder how they came to be.

Bryce Canyon, my favorite park

We finally arrived at one of my favorite Parks, Bryce National Park. I think I have been there at least a dozen times and I am awestruck from the time of my entering the park until I leave. I stand and look at all this beauty and I think of how many years it took to erode so much earth and let Mother Nature use her own imagination, designing all this beauty, and then leaving these colorful pinnacles standing for all to enjoy. All this beauty is found in what is, otherwise barren land. God has certainly worked overtime to give us such magnificent beauty. You can spend the complete day just visiting all the observation turnouts. Each overlook has its own beauty wrapped in splendid colors. There are a couple of arches down toward the end of the park and it is a must to travel to the end of the road before turning back.

Entering Zion.

Our next venture was into Zion National Park. Again, this park is very beautiful and entirely different from Bryce. Before entering the park you will descend several hundred feet, coming down into a canyon. You will go through several long tunnels while descending to the valley below.

One is the longest tunnel of any I have ever been through. I am not sure of the length but it is close to two miles. There are holes cut into the side of the wall to give some light but mainly to let fresh air enter the tunnel. There, again, you see beautiful rock formations and sheer solid rock walls.

If you observe closely, you will see rock climbers all along these sheer walls At the Visitors Center you have to leave your car (or bus) and take a tram, which takes you on a tour all the way through the park. This service is provided by the National Park and there is no charge for it. You are free to get off at any of the frequent stops and stay as long as you like. When you are ready to move on, just catch the next tram going the way you want to go. You can make a quick tour through the park by not getting off the tram or you can get off at every stop and make a day of it.

We left Zion and retraced our path for several miles so we could visit Cedar Breaks National Monument on the way into Cedar City for our next over night stop. Cedar Breaks is just another little Bryce Canyon. It is a very nice place to visit and it is close to Cedar City. It has the same colors and pinnacles that you will find in Bryce but on a smaller scale. By this time we have seen all the beautiful rock formations that we care to see. We are ready to head for home.

The next morning we take I-15 south toward Las Vegas and home. We arrived late in the afternoon at the Lodi Bus Depot where everyone will claim their suitcase for the final time on this trip and sleep in their own bed tonight.

This is an extremely hard life for a bus driver and I did the job. After all, someone had to do it.

Chapter 4

OPERATING A REGULAR SCHEDULE

Sometimes I would bid a regular Run, so I would have the same days off each week and go to work at the same hour each day. These were the advantages that working the extra board did not have. I could still take my request charters when they came up. While I was away on a charter, my run would be worked from the extra board until I returned.

My wife liked my being on a regular run because she could make definite plans for us to do things or go somewhere. When working the extra board, I was on call twenty-four hours a day. As soon as I thought I was going to be off for the day, I would surely be called in to work. You could never make definite plans as long as you worked the extra board but I loved the idea of doing something different every day. With my low seniority the first few years, the only runs I could hold were low paying and I could make more by working the extra board.

The last few years I drove for Greyhound, I did have the seniority to hold a high paying run and I wanted to build up my retirement so I stayed on a run.

The run I was on left the Stockton Depot at 3:30 PM and ended in San Francisco. Then I would get a fresh bus and take the Vancouver, B. C. schedule as far as Redding, California. I arrived in Redding at 11:20 PM and my day was finished. I would turn the tickets and the bus over to another driver, and he or she would take the bus on to Medford, Oregon and so on until the bus reached Vancouver, B. C.

We had a Dormitory above the Depot in Redding and I would immediately go up and go to bed. My schedule back to San Francisco left at 9:00 AM the next morning. It was a schedule that had originated in Vancouver, and I would take it to its final destination in San Francisco.

It took two drivers to handle the run I was on. I would meet the other driver in San Francisco on my way back to Stockton. He would have left on the 3:30 PM schedule that I had left the day before. We had an hour in San Francisco and we usually talked about what had happened since I had left Stockton.

I have always enjoyed people and I have never been at a loss for words when talking to them. However, the last few years, I was constantly having problems with the younger generation wanting to smoke pot on the bus. Smoking was confined to the last two rows of seats and to cigarettes only.

When I left the Stockton depot each trip I would make an announcement pertaining to smoking. I would hear some giggling in the rear of the bus and I knew I had some pot smokers aboard. I always wore sunglasses and adjusted the big rearview mirror in the bus, so I could see to the back of the bus without raising my head. I always kept the little six-inch window open by my side so it would create a draft and bring any smoke from the rear of the bus.

I usually got about five miles out of Stockton before I would smell marijuana. I immediately started looking to the rear and watching the kids (usually 16 to 20 years old) passing the marijuana around.

It was twenty miles to Tracy, my first stop, and by the time I arrived, I would have everyone that was involved with smoking, identified by clothing or looks. I would nonchalantly step off the bus and walk into the baggage room. I immediately picked up the phone and called the Tracy PD and in less than two minutes there would be two police cars and usually three, screeching to a halt surrounding the bus. I would then come out of the baggage room and greet the officers. I would go on the bus ahead of the officers and point out the ones I wanted removed.

The ones I had pointed out, were told by the officers,

"O.K., you heard the driver, he doesn't want you on his bus."

There would always be one of them saying, "But my mother is waiting for me in Oakland."

The officer would say, "You should have thought of that before smoking that weed."

It is one of our company rules to fill out an incident report, any time some one is ejected from our bus. This takes about an hour and we do it on our own time, without compensation. The second time this happened I quit filling out the reports. I had one boy tell me he would have my job by tomorrow.

I said, "Son, if I have to deal with people like you, you can have it."

I never filled out any more forms and never heard anything on any of these issues. I don't know what the Police did with those that left my bus, and truthfully, I never worried much about them. I never gave their tickets back to them either. This was one of the problems we faced every day on this schedule.

After reloading, I would pull out of the Tracy Depot and make the same announcement about smoking that I had made on leaving Stockton. I suppose I had made my point because from Tracy to San Francisco there was no smoking of any kind, not even a cigarette was smoked.

The same problem would happen again when I loaded in San Francisco for Vancouver. Usually nothing happened from S.F. to Oakland and Richmond. During this time no one smoked. This schedule made quite a few stops, as it was a local as far as Redding. I also had lots of commuters leaving S.F. going as far as Fairfield. It was usually after leaving

Fairfield that my pot smokers would come to life. On one occasion I had a big, older black fellow, start smoking pot just out of Richmond. He was sitting about halfway up in the bus. It is about thirty miles to my next stop so I pulled to the side of the freeway and went back to him and said,

"Sir, I just made an announcement about not smoking marijuana so please put it out."

He said, "You and who else is gonna make me?"

I am 6 ft. 4 inches tall, 220 pounds, and my word is usually taken with a little respect, but something told me it was not working this time and not to agitate this fellow any further.

I went back to the driver's seat and continued to the Fairfield Depot. When I got out of the bus I stood by the door as usual to help passengers off. A fellow that had been sitting behind me got off also and stood on the opposite side of the door. I fully expected the black fellow to come off the bus swinging at me, since he was getting off there. But he came out running and never looked back.

I said to the fellow standing opposite me, "I sure expected trouble when he got off."

The fellow standing by me said, "Driver I thought you had asked for more than you could handle back there, but you did the proper thing by leaving him alone."

Saying that, he pulled his jacket back to reveal a badge. He was a Detective with the SF Police Department and he commuted home with me every other day. He also said he was watching the incident and was ready to come to my aid if necessary. Needless to say that man did not have to buy a commute ticket after that. I also told the other driver working the other side of my run about what had happened and he rode free with him too. From that day on, I felt a little safer from SF to Fairfield.

My wife kept telling me I was either going to get knifed or shot by doing all this but I felt it was my responsibility to be in control. I never failed to have men and women get off the bus and tell me how much they appreciated my keeping the kids from smoking pot. They said that most of the drivers they had ridden with did not do it.

I personally have never smoked it and I disliked the smell of it when someone else is smoking it and therefore I would not allow it on my bus.

At the first part of my career, driving a bus, this was unheard of. Everyone was going to visit some one and they were always in a happy state of mind. Since I have retired, things have changed, there is no smoking at all on the buses, and that should eliminate all the problems I was having in the last few years that I drove.

My wife and I have life time passes to ride Greyhound anywhere in the USA or Canada, but we have never taken advantage of the opportunity to go somewhere together. The main reason, I suppose, is the fact we always need a car at our destination and I would rather drive my own car. My wife, De, has gone to the Seattle area a couple times alone, to visit her family.

I have covered almost every road in California, either on charters or on schedules. I have seen all the National Parks in the eleven Western States, plus driving the Alaska Highway, which is covered in another story in this book.

My life as a Greyhound Driver was a happy one and an educational one, geographically. I have seen many things that I would never have had the opportunity to see if I had not been behind the steering wheel of a Greyhound bus.

I did not know, when I was growing up, how important my driving record would be in my career. I suppose with the threat from my father, that I would never drive the family car if I had an accident that was my fault, or was seen horsing around with it, might have had a great influence on my safe driving.

I firmly believe the accident I was in when I joined the CMTC, at only sixteen years of age, had a lasting impression on me and had the greatest effect on my driving record. This was a totally avoidable accident, which caused the loss of one life, loss of the driver's arm and broken bones in all of the kids. I was the only one that did not have a broken bone.

We had safety seminars every two years that Greyhound held for all the drivers, and we were required to attend them. Greyhound even went so far as to pay our full run pay to be sure we attended. I never failed to benefit from what I learned there.

Greyhound says that accidents do not happen on their own, they are caused. I firmly believe, barring mechanical problems, that statement is true.

At one of the safety seminars the title of the program was:

"Always get the big picture."

I was very impressed with that program which meant:

Always know what is behind you, on both sides of you, and ahead of you. Not just down the road, but on each side of the road, and watch for roads crossing yours. If there is a stray cow grazing in a ditch, that cow may dart out as you get near.

You should never be surprised by any action. You should already be aware of the possibilities that someone might do the unexpected.

Get the big Picture! Leave yourself an escape path. Never stay along side another bus or large truck as that gives you a blind side and should the bus or truck loose a wheel or blow a tire you might find yourself in a heap of trouble.

The longer I drove buses, the more I learned of what to expect and how to keep my passengers safe. A gentleman riding my bus once told me that he could never handle my job. I asked why and he said there was too much responsibility with having all these passenger's lives in my hands.

I told him that I never worried about the lives of my passengers. As long as I protected myself they would also be safe. Remember, I would be the first to feel the impact of the windshield and that did not appeal to me.

I drove Greyhound buses for twenty-eight years without even a fender bender, and you do not do that without getting the BIG PICTURE.

During my time I could have had several accidents that were not my fault. Sometimes people seemed to challenge the buses, but it only takes a second to avoid them and give up the right of way, even if it is yours.

When I started my career with Greyhound, we held the record for being the safest drivers in the world. I don't give all that credit to the drivers, I give most of it to God, as He knows there are people aboard those buses, and He has helped me out several times.

There were 654 drivers working in my division when I started work for Greyhound. When I retired my seniority number was 56. I had come a long way in the twenty-eight years and would have liked to make it under the double-digit number before I retired. I retired at the age of sixty. I was planning to work until I was sixty-five but my career was cut short by a strike in 1983.

The strike lasted several months and I never returned to work when it was over. I was fired during the strike for criminal misconduct and they considered me dangerous to the public. I have explained the firing in more detail in another chapter in this book.

A Greyhound driver had a tough life sometimes, and I felt I was the one to do it.

Chapter 5

THINGS THAT HAPPENED ON REGULAR SCHEDULES

One day I had just left the Oakland depot on the way to San Francisco. A lady was sitting on the right front seat with her three-year old boy. Just before we came to the Toll Plaza, a huge area of the mud flats was showing out the right side of the bus, as the tide was out at the time. The little boy got very excited and started yelling,

"Mommy, Mommy, look at all the chickens!"

The mother then asked me why there were so many chickens out there. I laughed and said the "chickens" were actually sea gulls that were feeding on the marshland while the tide was out. This was their first time to California and they had never seen sea gulls like this in Tennessee.

***

One Sunday I was called to work at six o'clock in the evening. At that time we had a schedule originating out of Sacramento going to San Diego. The schedule was mostly for the benefit of servicemen returning from weekend leaves to the Navy base at San Diego. It arrived in San Diego around six the next morning giving the sailors time to get to the base without being AWOL.

When the schedule arrived in Stockton there was a second section already on it. We loaded a third bus and there were three people left over. At that time Greyhound would put on another bus even for one passenger. No one was ever left standing. The fourth section was assigned to me and I started loading the three people.

One passenger was a young girl in her late teens and a gentleman in his mid thirties. The last passenger was a sailor. He was slightly inebriated. Normally I would not have taken him but I only had two other passengers and since I would be going direct to Los Angeles, I told him if he would go to the rear of the bus and go to sleep he could go.

I went into the dispatch office and signed out and when I came back and stepped up in the bus the sailor was sitting in the seat across the aisle from the girl. I immediately walked back and reminded him of what I had told him. He went to the back seat.

I had only driven twenty or thirty miles down I-5 when I saw him coming up the isle and he sat down with the girl. I pulled the bus onto the shoulder of the road and turned on my flashers. I walked back to him and tapped him on the shoulder. He did not even realize we had stopped.

I said, "Fellow I am not going to tell you again. If you don't go to the back seat and stay there I will put you off the bus right here."

He saluted me and went to the rear of the bus and I never heard a word out of him the rest of the way. He was still sleeping when we arrived in Los Angeles.

I could have refused to take him back in Stockton but I knew he would be AWOL the next morning and since I only had two other passengers I took a chance with him. I did have a little trouble with him but it turned out fine in the long run.

***

One of Greyhounds policies was to leave it up to the driver as to whether we would take a person or not. We all knew from experience that if we took a drunk we would regret it.

He would usually throw up in the aisle or start using vulgar language.

To save a lot of unnecessary inconvenience for the other passengers and our selves, it was always best to leave the drunks at the depot.

***

One day I had gone into Sacramento on a schedule and I was cut off there. A bus had broken down near the Donner Summit. Sacramento was out of extra board drivers, so I was given an assignment to drive the mechanic to the bus so he could repair it and then he would drive it back. We arrived at the bus and the mechanic had it repaired in a very short time. We turned the buses around and started back to Sacramento. I was in the lead coming back and we had just gone through Auburn, California when we came upon a curve in the highway. My lights illuminated cars lying in the road. The road was blocked completely and I had no alternative but to go into the median. There were rocks about six inches in diameter to prevent people from making turns across the median. I thought I was losing control of the bus but managed to get it stopped. I was worried about the mechanic not seeing the cars and him running into them, Fortunately, he followed me into the median.

This happened about three A.M. and there was not much traffic. We both jumped out of our buses and started putting flares out along the roadway. There were five cars involved and people lying all over the road. Some were just coming to and starting to get up.

I can only imagine what would have happened had I been drowsy and run into this mess. There were several people still in the cars and were now starting to get out. Luckily a Highway Patrolman showed up almost immediately and took control of everything. After getting what information we could give him, he told us we could go.

After we got back to Sacramento the mechanic and I were talking over a cup of coffee and I told him I was so afraid he would run into the middle of all the mess because he could not see it. He said when I went into the median he thought at first I had gone to sleep but then I had gone in too fast so he knew there had to be a reason for it. After coffee the dispatcher gave me another bus and told me I could deadhead back to Stockton. What a night!

***

One winter day I was taking a gambling charter to Reno and it was snowing very hard over the Sierras. There was already three feet of snow on the ground and as we reached the top of the Donner Summit, we came upon a roadblock. It was about ten o'clock then and we sat there on the highway not being able to move until about three in the afternoon. We finally started moving slowly through the blizzard and we reached Reno about six that evening. Normally this is the time we should be loading up for our return trip. At this time all roads leading to the west out of Reno were closed. There were fourteen buses sitting in the Reno depot waiting to get back to California. The dispatcher finally put us to bed, as we were definitely not leaving that night when it was decided the roads would not open before noon the next day. I don't know what the passengers did all this time.

At noon the next day the roads were still closed and no word as to when they might be opened. My passengers along with thirteen other busses were overloading the depot.

Finally at six that evening the roads were not opened but the California Highway Patrol said they would release the fourteen buses to go into California by the way of the feather river highway (highway 70). We were to leave in a convoy and stay together. The road going north out Reno (395) had about a foot of snow on it and if it were not for the snow poles along the highway, we would have been at a total loss as to where the highway was. The past two days the road had

60

not been plowed and only a truck or bus could navigate it. The going was tough for the first bus, but all the others just stayed in his tracks. We arrived in Orville and we were all dead tired but there was nothing open for coffee so we continued to Yuba City. We found two restaurants open so we divided the buses among the coffee shops and if you can imagine fourteen buses converging on your café and you only having a minimum crew, then you know what the waitresses must have felt. I was ashamed to go in but I was in need of a cup of coffee. I am sure there were happy faces when the last bus departed.

We could only drive ten hours legally, without eight hours off, and most of us were reaching twelve hours of driving time. I do not remember just how I logged my time but I never got any repercussion from it. It was just one of those things and there was nothing we could do about it.

***

During holidays such as Christmas, we were always short of drivers. The extra boards were always out of men regardless of where you went. The dispatcher could put you to bed and after eight hours he would supplement you to his board and off you would go in a direction not toward your home terminal. I remember taking a third section of a Los Angeles schedule to Fresno. Normally, that would be as far as I would go as it was my division point but the dispatcher had no one to relieve me so I had to continue to Los Angeles. I was starting out fresh from Stockton so I could legally do it. When I got to L.A. the dispatcher put me to bed. Eight hours later I was called to double a schedule to Phoenix. This was not too bad as it was an express schedule and I could follow the first section.

When I got to Phoenix, I was put to bed again. Eight hours later I was called to cover a run back to L.A. Apparently the regular driver was sick and his run had to be covered off the extra board. An out-of-town extra board driver had first rights to anything going back toward his home terminal so I was assigned the run. Now I am the first section and have no idea where any of the depots are located. This schedule was a semi-local and that made it even worse for me. The dispatcher sent me off with his blessings and said not to worry, I would get there. That was easy for him to say.

I have never been so embarrassed in my life as I was when I stepped up in the bus. I decided I would be truthful with the passengers and I ask if some one that knew where the depots were would come up front and help me find our way, since I worked out of Stockton, California and had no idea of where we were going. There was a gentleman spoke up and said he would help me as far as Indio as that was as far as he was going and I said I could manage from there.

Some of our drivers from Stockton have gone as far as El Paso, Texas before starting back for their home terminal. Most of the schedules would be running three or four sections on Christmas Holidays. Normally we had enough drivers working but this is one business you cannot hire extra men just for the Holidays.

When Ft. Ord was still active, they would start releasing the boys to go home for Christmas about the fifteenth of December. They would start sending about twenty-five buses a day until all the boys were gone. We started moving every spare bus we had down to Ft. Ord the week prior to the big move. If you happened to get caught up in that operation, you did not know when you would get home. The first group of drivers sent out would drive their ten hours and be put to bed. Then when the next wave of buses came through, you were destined to go further from home.

It was really neat how they arranged where each bus would be going. There would be an Atlanta bus and everyone going to and beyond would board that bus. There would be one to New Orleans and so on. Once loaded the bus did not stop except for meal stops and driver changes. We got the boys home faster than any mode of transportation except flying.

There were buses going to every large city in the U.S.A. This only happened once a year thank God. I thought the travel arrangements to move all the boys out of camp so swiftly was a well planned operation between Greyhound and the Transportation Officers at Ft. Ord. All you needed to do was get on the right bus.

It was always a big surprise to all the drivers as to where they might end up. I even made it back home the next day, one year, but it was very unusual to be that lucky. Of course we made a very handsome pay check for that pay period every year, which made our wives more tolerant of our being gone, especially at Christmas time. All the drivers looked forward to the "Ft. Ord" moves each year.

***

Another operation we enjoyed each year was during the fire season in the summer. I am not saying I looked forward to seeing our National Forests burn, because that is not true. During the fire season Greyhound would be called upon to pick fire fighters up at the airport and transport them to the fire line in the mountains. Usually there would be two to five buses needed to move the fighters. The drivers would then be put on standby to move the fighters as needed. We were given sleeping bags and we ate with the fire crew. The only thing we had to do was stay by our buses, ready to move the fire fighters when needed. The base camps were usually located in a meadow and we would back our buses under the pine trees and either sleep or play cards. We would remain at the camp until the fire was over, then we would return the fire fighters to the airport. Sometimes we would be at the fire for weeks.

***

You would never believe the places we took those buses. You think of a Greyhound bus as a vehicle used only on freeways. We took them into places where we had to have a bulldozer pull us out. I had one bus hung up on rocks while trying to cross a stream. I even busted a radiator on one bus while trying to negotiate a small concrete bridge. We were in places not meant for Greyhound buses.

Every summer there would be a three bus charter originating from the First Baptist Church in Lodi to take their kids to a church camp at Hume Lake located in Kings Canyon National Park. If you were working the extra board you stood a good chance of catching one. I caught them several years and it was always an enjoyable trip. The dispatcher always told us where we were going so we always threw in a pair of trunks and we would go for a swim in the lake before we left for home. We would go to Fresno and take highway 180 to the east for eighty miles and we would be at an altitude of about 6,500 feet. There were camps there where churches could send their kids for a couple weeks during the summer. After unloading the kids, instead of starting for home, we took the buses around to the opposite side from the camp and put on our trunks in the bus and then went for a swim for thirty minutes. It was quite a relief to cool off before driving back down into the hot valley. I always enjoyed catching one of the Hume Lake trips.

Kings Canyon and Sequoia National Park are next to each other and are beautiful places to visit and see some of the largest redwood trees. I have since driven my wife down to visit both parks.

After having seen all the National Parks in the western U.S.A, I can still enjoy visiting them again and sharing them with my wife.

Chapter 6

PLEASE, DOES ANYBODY HEAR ME?

The life of a Greyhound Bus Driver is an interesting one. You meet lots of different people, some with good attitudes and some with attitudes that are indescribable here. Most of them are in the happy mode though, because they are going some place exciting, visiting relatives, seeing old friends.

It was with this kind of group that I arrived in Reno, Nevada on a schedule from San Francisco to N.Y.C. on a beautiful spring day. Everyone was happy, some getting off because they live there, some getting off the bus to gamble while there and some would be returning to the bus to continue east to distant points. Everyone must get off the bus though, as this is a scheduled meal stop. The bus will be refueled, cleaned inside, and the restroom will be serviced. This is my division point, so I will be leaving the bus, also. I go into the driver's room and turn my tickets over to the dispatcher. He then hands the tickets to another driver for the continuation of the bus to New York City.

There will be a driver change at Elko, Nevada, Salt Lake City and points along the way. Each segment to NYC will be driven with a fresh driver, but the same bus will go the full distance.

I go upstairs to the dormitory. At each Division point we have our own dormitory above the depot with at least a dozen quiet air conditioned private rooms where the drivers can sleep undisturbed and get the required rest before making his or her return to their home terminal. My home terminal is Stockton, California.

In going upstairs to my room, I ran into another driver friend that also works out of Stockton. He was getting ready for his return to San Francisco and then home. He and I were both single at the time, each having gone through a divorce.

I asked what he had planned for his vacation that summer, since mine was coming up soon. Carl's mother and most of his family lived in Sallisaw, Oklahoma. Since I hadn't made definite plans for my vacation and having never been in Oklahoma, I suggested we take my plane and fly back there for a couple of weeks and visit his family.

I couldn't have said anything that would have pleased Carl more when I mentioned flying back in my plane. We started planning the trip immediately.

May 13, 1977 we left the Lodi Airport in my Cessna 172, bound for Sallisaw, Oklahoma. At the time Carl was not too familiar with small airplanes and I think he had doubts, at first, of ever seeing his mother again. He had flown with me a few times before but the flights were of short duration and he had no concept of how we could ever find our way across all that open country, with no sign posts showing us the way. We got as far as Hobbs, New Mexico without incident. Then the air became so turbulent that even I started to yell uncle. Our straight through flight was now becoming questionable, and after a brief discussion, we landed and spent the night in Hobbs.

I might add that the air usually gets very turbulent in the afternoon when flying in the desert country, especially if there are storms anywhere nearby. It is always a wise decision to plan your flights in the morning and be on the ground around lunchtime to obtain a smoother ride.

About four the next morning I awakened and noticed the wind had died down, so I suggested we leave at that time in order to get a better ride on into Sallisaw. We took a taxi out to the airport and found the plane in the transient parking area. I have never seen such total darkness at any airport. I took my flashlight and did a preflight on the plane. Then I got in and started the engine and was ready to taxi out for departure. I had no idea which way to go. I thought the airport tower was closed during the night hours and I was deeply in need of help in getting to the runway. I gave the tower a call, fully expecting to get no answer, but to my surprise a voice come back with,

"You need some lights down there?"

The tower said since they had so little traffic during the night, they only turn the lights on as needed. Now there were lights everywhere, we followed the blue taxi lights to the active runway and we were soon on our way.

As we departed Hobbs, we could see lightening flashing continually in the east, toward the Midland, Texas area. The air was smooth though and we had a thirty-five mile per hour tail wind and that boosted our ground speed considerably. We had this tailwind for the remainder of the trip. What more could we ask for at this time. We arrived in Sallisaw two hours earlier than my flight plan called for. There was that much difference in the extra speed the tailwind had given us.

Except for the weather, we spent a very relaxing and comfortable two weeks in Sallisaw. The first night we were there we endured a tornado, rain, hailstorm and all sorts of things the Oklahoma "Weather Gods" could throw at us. This was the same storm we had watched as we were leaving Roswell that morning.

I was more concerned about leaving my plane tied down at the airport than I was for my own safety during the tornado that passed nearby the first night. Since it was our ride home, I was very concerned about what might have happened to the plane and I could hardly wait to get to the airport the next morning to check on it.

The morning after the storm I hurried to the airport and was relieved to find the plane in one piece with no apparent damage. It did not appear to have even bounced around much. It did have the protection, though, of a large hanger blocking the storm, for which I was very thankful.

It was decided all of Carl's family would go down on the river for a picnic and the boys could fish. As I remember, we did not do too well as fishermen. In fact I do not recall either of us catching any fish at all. That didn't matter though, as we had gone to the river with Carl's family for a picnic anyway. We decided after we didn't catch any fish, we would go swimming instead and let the fish live another day. We put away our gear and joined his family. Carl and I were the only ones that had tried fishing. We had lots of fun though, combining fishing with the picnic.

We soon found that lying in green grass and walking through brush, one soon becomes infested with chiggers and a few ticks. Being from California, it had been a long time since I had had the privilege of getting acquainted with these little "buggars." We had them in Texas when I was growing up but I had since forgotten about them. I would have preferred not to become reacquainted.

Life is at a much slower pace there in Sallisaw and I don't know when I have enjoyed a more relaxing vacation. It gave me a chance to see life being lived like it should be. No one seemed to ever get in a hurry for anything. After all, there is tomorrow and even the next day if need be. Our best entertainment in the evening was to sit out in the front yard and watch the old rooster make every hen around the yard before they all flew up in the trees to roost. What a rooster!

That is the kind of living I can remember while growing up in Texas. In California my life seemed to be going at top speed most of the time with no time to stop and smell the roses. While there I was able to sit and watch the grass grow without feeling guilty. What a life!

All good things have to end sometime and we found the day had arrived to begin our journey home only to soon. Everyone went to the airport to see us off, and after taking all (that wanted to go) for an airplane ride, we said goodbye and departed Sallisaw.

The first leg of our trip toward home was flown above a solid cloud layer. There was an occasional break in the clouds but most of the time there was a solid layer below us. Our first fuel stop was Abilene, Texas. By the time we arrived in Abilene, the clouds had broken and we were into clear weather. We got out of the plane and stretched our legs and took a walk around the plane while the tanks were being topped and then we were ready to continue our flight. We boarded the plane again and we were on our way, heading for El Paso, Texas.

Leaving Sallisaw

Coming straight in from the east, the El Paso tower cleared me to land on runway 22. This runway is over 11,000 ft. long and I landed on the end of the runway as I usually do, then losing sight of the airport, I decided to lift off again and stay airborne for a while instead of taxiing all the way to the turn-off at the terminal. The east-west runway in El Paso has the longest runway I ever landed on. Biggs Air Force Base is adjacent to the El Paso International and they use this runway for some of their flights also.

After topping the fuel tanks again, we departed for Tucson, Arizona. Seems like we were constantly topping off the tanks but fuel is what keeps the windmill turning on the front of the plane, and without it turning, you don't go anywhere!

On arriving in Tucson, (a scheduled overnight stop) we took a swim in the motel pool. It was a warm day and the swim was very refreshing. We then had dinner with plenty of time to gather our thoughts about the trip and enjoy the weather at hand. The weather in Tucson always seems to be perfect this time of year.

There was a nice motel right on the airport property in Tucson, so it was very convenient for flyers passing through to find close accommodations. The FBO (fixed base operator) took us to the motel even though it was only a few steps away.

At airports where there are no motels on the field, (which there are very few), you will find a list of motels on the wall by the phone located in the office. Usually all you had to do was pick up the phone and push a button on the motel of your choice (saves trying to remember the number), and these motels that were listed would have a courtesy van come to pick you up and return you to your plane the next morning. That makes air travel very convenient and worry free.

We checked out of the motel, had breakfast, fueled the plane and were sitting on the end of the runway 29R at 8 A.M., waiting for permission to take-off.

The day was one of those days you only dream about, with very little wind and as the temperature had not started its climb yet, it had the making of a beautiful day. Visibility was severe clear, you could see forever. The aroma of new mown grass with a tint of sage, drifted through the open window on my side of the cabin. This made me want to park the plane, get out and run into the middle of the field, lay down on my back and soak in all this sweet smell and beauty that mother nature was offering us. Nothing can be so inspiring as Arizona in the springtime.

However, life goes on and the tower's voice brought me back to reality.

"78 Niner one Tango, cleared for take-off, with a left hand turnout."

"Thank you tower, 78 Niner one Tango is rolling." I replied.

We were on our way to Palms Spring.

This was a day you were just happy to be living, and to be flying in your own aircraft made it even more enjoyable. We had reached our cruising altitude and were flying along, deep in our own thoughts, enjoying a very smooth ride at 8,500 ft. with not a care in the world when all of a sudden a terrible load was placed upon my shoulders.

Only an hour had passed since leaving Tucson when I began to notice some clouds building up in the west along our route. I didn't expect them to give us any trouble but I decided to give flight service a call anyway and get an update on the weather.

There are remote transmitters located through out the desert, so one can contact flight service almost anywhere you might be flying. These sites are monitored 24 hours a day.

It was while I was dialing in the number for flight service that I was shaken by a frantic voice crying out:

"PLEASE, does anybody hear me?"

My first thought was, "Fellow, you are using the wrong frequency." Then it dawned on---me like a bolt of lightening. This guy is in trouble!

I responded with, "I hear you loud and clear, how can I help you?"

"This is 82 Charlie and I am lost," came his terrifying reply.

My first impulse was to ask where he was but then he would not be lost if he knew where he was.

Instead I ask, "Where did you depart this morning?"

"I left Tucson at eight this morning and I was going to Phoenix," was his reply. "I should have been there already but I don't see anything but desert."

"What type of aircraft are you flying, and how much fuel do you have on board," I asked.

"I am flying a C-172 and I had full tanks when I left Tucson," he said.

I told him I was also flying a C-172 and I had left Tucson at eight. Since we had been flying about one hour, we still had about three or more hours flying time left before running low on fuel and I promised to have him located before he used all his fuel.

Knowing I could lose communication at any time, I was desperate to help this poor guy. His voice was beginning to show panic and you can't begin to imagine what it is like to be lost in an airplane in this situation.

Panic in a plane is so severe and immediate. Pilots have actually flown their planes into the ground by freezing at the controls. It is like having a nightmare, a dream of falling off a cliff and being lucky enough to grab a bush to hang on---

then have the bush break off, sending you plummeting into the depths.

In a car you simply pull off the road and solve any immediate problem. In an airplane your choices are few. You do not have time to park and think this thing over. You have to make an immediate decision. So panic is the least favored one of your options, and it comes quickly, automatically, without help from anyone.

I knew my time was limited before I lost communication with him. I began to perspire profusely and told him to stand by. I made contact with flight service and told them we had a problem.

I was handed off to Albuquerque Center, as they control the area to the left of my course and flight service wanted to clear their frequency. I explained the situation to Albuquerque Center and they wanted to locate my position first.

Center gave me a number, 3575, to squawk in my transponder (a radar unit in my plane) so I could be positively identified and they would have my location.

Immediately Center said, "Radar contact 78 Niner One Tango, Victor 94, seventeen northwest of the Gila Bend VOR. Have 842 Charlie squawk 3576 and switch to this frequency."

On returning to the flight service frequency, I found him pleading again,

"Please, some body, help me."

If that doesn't jump-start your heart, then nothing will. I felt the over-whelming responsibility for making sure this fellow came out of this situation alive, and the burden rested on my shoulders alone. I felt so helpless. All the time I kept imagining each transmission would be the last one I would ever hear from him. I was his only lifeline. I could visualize him going the opposite direction, heading south into Mexico, only to crash in the mountains and never be found until years later. However his transmissions were remaining strong and that gave me hope for him.

All this time, Carl, listening through his headset, had not said a word. I can only imagine why. At the onset of our trip, he was probably thinking the same thing was going to happen to us. He could not understand, without following an Inter-state highway, how we would ever reach Sallisaw, Oklahoma. I told him we actually had our own Inter-state highways in the sky that we navigate on, but he could never see one.

Actually I was so occupied with my immediate problem that I had temporally forgotten all about Carl.

When 842C finally stopped his transmission, I gave him a call and told him to please trust me. I would not leave him stranded. I was going to be there for him until he was safely located. I told him I had been in contact with Albuquerque Center and they were, at this minute, gearing up to find him.

I told him Center wanted him to change to one of their frequencies at that time. They needed to clear the flight service frequency.

"Take your pencil and copy this number down, and then dial it into your transmitter, then I will go to that frequency and give you a call, O. K?"

The instructions I gave sounded simple enough for anyone to understand. I gave him plenty of time to change the frequency and then I dialed in the numbers and gave him a call. I waited and then repeated my call. No answer?

I went back down to the original frequency for flight service, only to find him frantically calling for help. Apparently he was so stricken with panic that he had lost all his ability to concentrate on his radio. He was so terrified of taking the chance of changing frequencies on his transmitter and losing his only contact with another human being. Or else his mind had already started going blank and he was losing his ability to comprehend anything being said to him.

I moved back to Centers frequency and told them I had relayed their message but to no avail. They would have to make contact on 842 Charlie's frequency since this man had lost all his ability to follow my instructions and I feared the worst for him.

Center concurred with me and said,

"Have him start climbing and keep up a steady conversation and try to calm him down some, until we pick him up on radar."

I relayed the message to 842 Charlie and told him they needed to know his altitude.

After a moment he said, "1500 feet."

At that altitude his transmissions could not be heard by anyone farther away than twenty or thirty miles because of the mountains surrounding him. Since I was at 8,500 ft. my transmissions could be heard well.

I don't know why I neglected to ask sooner. I could have had him start climbing at the onset of this encounter. Maybe I temporarily went into shock myself when our conversation first started and I felt the responsibility of helping him.

It was just a matter of time now before Center, while monitoring this frequency, would start seeing 842 Charlie's blip on their radar and be able to see his location and direct him back to the Gila Bend airport.

I continued talking to 842 C, telling him Center was monitoring our conversation and the moment they could hear him they would break-in.

I told him I was going to California and I asked what his destination was. He said he was going to Phoenix. We talked for several minutes and I kept his mind off his problem by asking questions and keeping my conversations short so I could try to judge any improvement in his voice. I kept asking his altitude and he was continuing to climb and was now up to five thousand feet.

All of a sudden Center cut in and told me to please stand-by as they were picking up a target.

Center then directed a message to me, "For your information, 78 Niner One Tango, the target is two miles off your right wing tip going the same direction as your flight."

Center began calling, "November 842 Charlie, Do you copy?"

Please God... make him answer!

Then it happened.

"This is 842 Charlie and I read you loud and clear," came 842 Charlie's voice.

"THANK YOU GOD," I said to myself.

Albuquerque Center told him they would get him back to the Gila Bend airport and for him to land, have a soda, and get himself composed before flying anymore.

Once radar and radio communication between the two had been firmly established, Center said, "842 Charlie, turn left to a heading of 120."

After a few minutes Center asked if he had turned to the new heading of 120.

"Yes," was 842 Charlie's reply.

"842 Charlie turn to a new heading of 080," Center said.

Moments later Center called 842 Charlie and told him he was now flying the correct heading for Gila Bend airport, fifteen miles, dead ahead.

"Report seeing the airport." Center said.

"By the way, for your information 842 Charlie, your compass is off 40 degrees," reported Center.

Wheeee!

What a relief to get this burden off my shoulders, out of my mind, my nerves and whatever else there was that I could unload. I cannot remember a time in my life when I was so jubilant for having accomplished a mission as demanding as this one had turned out to be.

All of a sudden, in a cheerful voice, I had not been accustomed to hearing, 842 Charlie told Center he had the airport in sight. At that time, he asked Center to thank me for my help.

"I think the man is still on this frequency, why don't you thank him yourself," replied Center.

Then 842 Charlie gave me a call and expressed his gratitude for all my help, and I knew it came from his heart, as his voice reflected it. I accepted his thanks and wished him many days of trouble free, happier flying.

I suppose you might say this incident was all in a days work, but I look at it differently. I think I was purposely put in that particular place at that time to be instrumental in the rescue of this person.

I wish to take no praise or recognition for this rescue. I know he would have done the same for me, as would anyone else that happened to be there at the time. For once I was at the right place at the right time and I thank God for his help in letting me be there.

Carl was very nervous and said, "We are probably lost now,"

I had not been paying any attention to where I was flying. I really hadn't paid attention for the last twenty minutes. I had just kept the plane headed in a westerly direction. I knew I was off course but I could remedy that situation in a very few minutes. Surprisingly, I was not that far off course and I knew the vicinity we were in and within minutes I had us back on course. My compass was set properly, and in a short time we were back on that big Inter-state (V94) in the sky.

After a half hour of quietness, with Carl and I both reliving the terrifying encounter of near tragedy, in our own thoughts, the headset crackled with Center's voice,

"78 Niner One Tango, are you still on frequency?"

"Yes." I replied.

"I am going to give you credit for one life saved, as I do believe, beyond any doubt, that without your help this man would never have made it. Have a good flight home." Center said to me.

***

After arriving back at the Lodi airport, and putting the plane to rest in the hanger, I had time to relive this incident in my mind many times and have tried to decide what happened on that frightful day. First of all, the voice was that of a young man, (eighteen to twenty), and I think he was just learning to fly. I believe this was his first solo cross-country trip.

In all aircraft we have a magnetic compass located in the top (or in) the middle of the instrument panel, or hung from the top of the windscreen. Then usually, directly in front of you, on the instrument panel, will be a gyrocompass, which we use to fly by as it is dampened, (slower to react in turning) and will not jump around like the magnetic compass will. The Gyro must be manually set to the proper magnetic heading at the start of each flight. When you align your plane with the runway for take off at each airport, you should make a practice of setting the gyrocompass with that runway heading. While in flight, you should reset the Gyro with the magnetic compass every twenty minutes or so to maintain accuracy, as the Gyro does have a tendency to drift some.

The numbers on all runways are not just numbers drawn out of a hat. They are the true magnetic compass headings, minus a zero. For example; runway 22 would be a 220 degree, magnetic heading. Runway 09 would be a 090 degree, magnetic heading. Always add a 0 to the runway number and you have the true magnetic compass heading of the runway.

When you shut down your aircraft after a flight, the gyrocompass may even spin for awhile before stopping, and consequently will not give you a correct reading without being manually reset.

I truly believe on that fateful morning in Tucson, when 842 Charlie had his plane aligned with runway 29L or 29R, (parallel runways, right and left) he must have ignored the gyrocompass. This being his first solo cross-country, he was nervous and excited about flying to Phoenix all alone. He then neglected to set the gyrocompass before take-off, and after becoming airborne his eyes drifted to the gyrocompass and he started navigating by it. Being forty degrees off to the left, naturally, would have put him on a course almost parallel with my flight path, and being that close to me, his transmissions remained loud and clear.

***

I have several regrets that will never be resolved from that trip:

One, during all the time I was talking to him, I neglected to ask him for his name.

Two, my major regret is my not taking the time to turn around and go back to Gila Bend and land, meet the young man and shake his hand. It would have only delayed me, possibly two hours at the most. Now I will never know exactly what happened but I am pretty sure my guess was right.

I guess you might say I was in a semi-state of panic during the time it took to rescue his person. That would explain why I didn't ask the crucial questions that I should have before I contacted Flight Service. I am only too happy to report, mission accomplished.

***

Just an after thought---Carl must have been impressed with our trip by private plane because the week after we returned he signed up and started his flying lessons. He went on to get his private pilot's license, and now he understands all about navigating the Super Hi-ways in the sky.

Chapter 7

DRIVING THE ALASKA HIGHWAY

The life of a Greyhound Bus Driver can be exciting and adventurous quite often during his career. One of my most exciting trips came on June 20th, 1971, when the dispatcher informed me that I had been requested by the Lodi Travel Club to drive their chartered bus to Alaska.

WOW---All my life, just hearing the word "ALASKA," had always intrigued me. Now I actually had the chance to go there. Our departure date was June 24th.

That is only four days away.

When a group chartered a Greyhound bus for a ball game, or a trip of any kind, they could request the driver of their choice. If a group has had a previous driver they liked, that had treated them well, they usually requested him to drive their next trip.

I had driven the Lodi Travel Club on several occasions and I suppose they liked my driving and the way I treated them. I have always made a habit of standing by the door, as people were exiting the bus, (actually it was company policy to do so) in case someone stumbled or fell. It was my habit to always take the women by the hand, giving them a feeling of security when stepping off the bus. Little things, like giving more attention to each individual's need was very important. For instance, I paid more attention and gave more of my time to an elderly person or someone with a disability. I treated them, as I would like to be treated, if I were in their shoes.

This is what makes a trip enjoyable for the group, and if a driver treated them in such a manner, he was usually requested to drive all their trips. That is how I became the regular driver for the Lodi Travel Club.

Just four days to get ready. As this was an eighteen-day trip, I had to buy more underwear, launder all my uniform shirts, (I ironed my own shirts with military creases), and have all my trousers cleaned.

WOW! I suppose there is no need to say that I was excited at this time, I took the last two days off to be sure to have everything ready. I double-checked everything to make sure I had all the clothing that I would need. I had heard of other drivers going on charters, and the first day out, they found their wife had packed eight tee shirts but no shorts. Having the sole responsibility for packing all of the clothing I would be wearing on this trip, I even triple checked.

WOW! ---I'm going to drive the Alaska Highway---I am going to Alaska.

Greyhound usually had many chartered buses going to Alaska during the summer months and each bus carried with it, a special "Alaska Kit." These packages contained, extra fan belts, spare headlamps, fuses and items that you would be hard pressed to find along the road, should a need for them arise. My bus contained such a package. The bus had just arrived the night before, from the San Francisco shop. The air conditioner was overhauled, new brakes were installed, all tires were replaced with new ones and the bus was serviced completely. It was then deadheaded to Stockton, especially for my charter.

On the morning of June 24th, I was at the depot a little early, double-checking the bus and all the equipment that I should have aboard. I had everything checked and ready to pull out well before the appointed time.

WOW! ---The day has come, and I was on my way to Lodi to pick up the group that would be my family for the next eighteen days. When I pulled into the Lodi depot, it was loaded with people and baggage. I began loading baggage. All the baggage would have to be handled by me, twice a day, for the next eighteen days. This was part of my job and I loaded it without giving it any more thought.

The Lodi group was made up of retired people enjoying their golden years to the fullest. Their ages ranged from the sixties and seventies and a few being in their eighties. Usually it is the same ones that made all the trips. The bus holds thirty-eight passengers but the Tour Director preferred to keep the rear three seats vacant. So we always had thirty-five people including the Tour Director on each of her trips.

Lodi Travel Club loading for Alaska

When everyone was onboard, I stepped up into the bus and made a brief announcement.

"This probably looks like a greyhound bus, and it may very well be, but for the next eighteen days it is going to be your private car and I am going to be your personal chauffeur. Should anyone want to stop and look at something along the way, just let me know and we will stop and all take a look. Now enjoy your trip."

With that said, we were on our way to Alaska.

We spent the first night in Portland and the next day, we rolled across Washington State and entered Canada, just out of Sumas, Washington. Our second night was spent in the Harrison Hot Springs Lodge, on the beautiful shores of Harrison Lake. This is just off Trans-Canada Highway 1. We then worked our way up through Kamloops, Williams Lake, and Prince George. Finally we arrived in Dawson Creek to spend the night before tackling the mighty Alaska Hi-way. It was then called the Alcan Highway, as it was a joint venture between the United States and Canada to provide a faster route into Alaska during World War Two.

It was in Dawson Creek that I encountered a "belligerent" signal light. I had to park the bus parallel to the curb in front of the hotel, which was near the corner of an intersection. As I was backing into the curb, I could see nothing behind or near me on my right rear side. However, just as I put on my brakes, I heard some glass breaking. I got out and walked to the rear of the bus and saw nothing. On a closer look I was astounded to see I had backed into a signal light.

This light was on a long curved arm extending out and down into the street. It was high enough that I could not see the arm reaching over into the street through my right side mirror. It was hidden behind the bus.

It had broken the curved rear window, luckily behind the rest room. I did not see any physical damage to the signal light so I did not bother to report it. I knew I had to get the window replaced as we were just getting ready to start the Alaska

Highway, which was all gravel and there would be lots of dust.

There were no provisions for a rear window in the Alaska Kit so I found a garage and the mechanic improvised a window out of a heavy wax cardboard and it served the purpose very efficiently and it looked good. I never mentioned the window when I got home and nothing was ever said about it. It was probably not noticed for quite a while.

This incident really tore my heart out though, as this was the first and only accident I had in the twenty-eight years of my driving for Greyhound. I do not really consider that as an accident.

It was only a few miles out of Dawson Creek that I realized there would be no more paved road until we crossed the Alaskan border. The Alaska Hi-way stretches 1523 miles from Dawson Creek to Fairbanks, Alaska.

The gravel was smoother than I expected. I was able to maintain 50 to 60 miles per hour and no one could possibly pass me as I was creating so much dust I could not see the road behind me. Some sections of the road were like a washboard and very rough.

I was told that each road crew along the highway had the responsibility for maintaining forty or fifty miles of the road. Some of the crews took pride in their work and wanted to be known for having the smoothest section of roadway along the entire highway. Others didn't care and that was the reason for the rough sections along the way.

I soon found I should slow down and move as far right as possible when meeting a truck (of which there were many), due to the flying gravel that most certainly would be following. My windshield had cracks and spider webs all over it.

I soon became proficient in ducking each time I saw a rock coming toward me from a passing vehicle. There was lots of truck traffic as most food items were trucked in rather than being shipped by boat.

The Lodi Travel Club was accustomed to stopping for coffee about ten o'clock in the morning on their trips, and soon someone yells from the rear of the bus.

"Grady, where are we stopping for coffee this morning?"

I replied, "I think we will be lucky to find a place for lunch." (I am only joking of course). I thought!

Dust in rear view mirror

About ten thirty, we came upon a small two-pump service station that had a sign reading, "Restaurant." Here is what we were looking for! I pull the bus into the driveway and we all got out. Inside the, "Restaurant," there were three stools at a six foot counter. Needless to say no one had lunch. We did however; clean out his candy and cracker jars, and the few small potato chip packages, (which had probably been there for years) since that was all he had that was edible. That was our coffee and lunch stop combined. Farther down the highway we saw a sign advertising a restaurant and lodge on a lake so I turned into a narrow road, (wondering if I had made a mistake) but finally we arrived at the lodge. It looked large enough to handle us, and by gosh, here comes a man running out to show me where to park.

Coffee break

Only this man had no intentions of parking me, he wanted to turn me around and head me back to the highway. They did not have food to serve us, and he let me know that in no uncertain words. He would not let anyone get off the bus.

Well, that was the way our first day went, without coffee or lunch. We finally arrived in Ft. Nelson for an overnight stop. I unloaded the baggage and found it was covered with a heavy layer of dust. It was hard to distinguish even the color of each piece. Everyone got to their room and settled in. Since there were no facilities at the motel for eating, I told the group I would drive them to a restaurant for dinner. In the meantime, I had talked to the owner of the motel and had asked him what were the chances of finding a place to eat, the next day. He asked which way I had come, and before I could answer, he said it didn't really matter, as there were no facilities going either direction.

There are fairly large cities about every three hundred miles, or just a good days drive. There was little if anything to be found at that time and probably is about the same way now.

I took the group to dinner and after bringing them back to the motel, I drove back into town and found a large grocery store. I bought bread, (I counted the slices in a loaf) and enough canned luncheon meat for one sandwich each, plus some mixed fresh fruit, cookies and cans of fruit juice. I packed all this in a large box and the grocer helped me tape it securely so the dust could not get in, as it would have to be placed in the baggage bin.

The next morning I loaded the baggage and the group without mentioning the food I had stored, and we got under way. I was all set for the first heckler to ask me about where we would be having lunch. Sure enough, down the road someone says,

"Grady, are we going to have to go without lunch again today?"

"No," I said, "We are going to find a nice lake and I am going to pull the bus down by the shoreline and we are going to have a picnic."

Of course there was a lot of laughter, and a lot of doubt and disbelief. We had been passing a lot of beautiful lakes and I was just waiting for the right one. I needed one where I could leave the highway, where the ditch along the road was shallow, and with trees far enough apart to get the bus down to the lake. Around noontime I came upon the perfect lake. It had easy access to leave the road and had a hard surface all the way to the lake. I slowed the bus and left the roadway. I made my way slowly through the trees and parked along side the lake.

"Can I get some of you women to give me a hand?' I asked as I stood up.

No one moved. They just sat looking down the aisle at me.

"Hey," I said, "I promised you a picnic by the lake, and here we are."

I got off the bus, opened the baggage bin containing the food box, and when I pulled it out and started opening it, everyone started coming to life. I never saw a more jubilant crowd. It was the first time anyone had ever seen a Greyhound bus parked off the pavement, especially sitting alongside a lake in the wilderness. We enjoyed our picnic and after a walk alongside the lake, we boarded the bus again for Watson Lake.

I was talking to an elderly gentleman in our group and he mentioned that he had a self-winding watch, and many times while he was at home, it would run down from lack of his movement. But he said, as he put his hand on my shoulder, "You have shore kept that spring wound tight the last couple days."

On arrival at Watson Lake, we continued thru town about a half mile to an area known as the "Sign Posts." This all started back when the road was being constructed. Someone put up a sign from his hometown indicating the mileage to it, and then another was put up until there were literally hundreds of City Limit signs stuck on poles, and you can still see them today.

The famous Watson Lake signposts

The night at Watson Lake was repetitious of the night before. Only this time I had to look for a fueling station. Greyhound had given me a list of all the places where I was authorized to get fuel, by just signing my name and giving them my charter and bus number.

A greyhound bus is good for about 1100 miles before having to take on fuel. You have to keep an accurate account of miles driven each day so that you never run out, since there is no fuel gauge on any of the buses. Each bus contains its own fuel card and it is the responsibility of each driver to put in the mileage he has driven at the end of his or her shift so that an accurate mileage record is available to the next driver.

By the time I did my chores and had gotten back to the motel I was tired, but there was plenty of daylight left, it was only ten-thirty. I was ready to turn in but it was still daylight outside and I cannot sleep with so much daylight. I turned in anyway, as I needed my rest and I was tired, regardless of what time of day it appeared to be. I had closed the drapes on the window and found it to be very uncomfortable with no air circulating. Since we had no air conditioner in the rooms, I decided to open the drapes. There I lay in my shorts with the window wide open and in broad daylight in view of any one walking by my window at eleven o'clock at night. I was so tired I simply said to heck with it and turned over and went to sleep.

The next day was a copy of the day before. We were seeing the same little trees and lots of lakes. The road was beginning to be repetitious, it's over hill and over dale, no hills over 1800 feet along the road. I was told the trees do not grow very large, because of the permafrost.

I was cruising along about fifty or so miles per hour when I saw a rain shower crossing the road up ahead. I did not slow down, and when I hit the wet area, the bus went every which way but the way I wanted it to go. I let off on the throttle but did not touch the brakes and with a lot of help from God, we got the bus under control. It was a very exciting few minutes for everyone and I learned another lesson that day. The Alaska Highway is made up of a very heavy clay content and it becomes so slippery when it is wet that it requires very careful maneuvering, It was very fortunate that I was able to get the bus under control.

I learned a very critical lesson that day, slow down before I approach the wet surface if I see another rain shower up ahead.

We arrived in Whitehorse in the early evening so we had plenty of time for some sightseeing and exploring. One of the old paddle wheel steamers used during the gold rush days sits on display on the river in downtown Whitehorse. This is also the beginning of the narrow gauge railroad, which goes across the mountain to Skagway, where thousands of gold seekers first came into the heart of Alaska. Some rode the train, but most everyone walked over a well-worn trail.

When we left Whitehorse the next morning, we left the Alaska hi-way and made a right turn, which would take us to the historic town of Dawson City. When we arrived in Dawson, we had to split the group. There were no facilities that could handle thirty-six people so we had to use two motels. The city is made up mostly of the original buildings built during the gold rush days.

One of the two Hotels

The wooden buildings, minus paint, are very well preserved and there are still boardwalks in some areas. We attended an old Vaudeville theater (built in the gold rush days) the first night, and saw performances that took us back to the days of the gold rush and those of scantily clad dancing girls. It was a memorable visit and a very interesting one, just sight seeing and walking thru the main part of town, knowing history was made here. Some of the group did souvenir shopping while others just walked and browsed through stores. Visiting Dawson took us off the Alaska Highway as it was to our right on the way toward Fairbanks, but it was very much worth the time and extra mileage

When we left town the next day, we had to take a ferry to cross the Yukon River. We could see the ferry across the river a couple hundred yards up stream. We sat on the loading ramp waiting for it to come over and get us. As the ferry left the other side, it took a fast turn down stream with the current, but as it became even with us it turned and started toward the ramp.

Ferry coming to take us across the Yukon.

Once the ferry was securely tied up to the ramp, they motioned me aboard. Actually the ferry looked as if our bus would make it sink, and I was relieved once they had me safely parked on the extreme right side of the barge.

But then they loaded a huge semi truck, up close, on my left side. I really had my doubts, along with the passengers, whether ferry was going to float. But after a lot of squeaks and groans, the ferry began moving out into the current. (I just knew the water was going to be mighty cold). The cable we were attached too became taut and after a brief struggle with the current of the mighty Yukon, we were soon unloading on the other side, without anyone getting wet.

Shortly we joined the Alaska Highway again, and a few miles down the road we arrived at Tok Junction. At Tok, the highway divides, the road to the left goes to Anchorage and the one to the right goes to Fairbanks. We took the one to Fairbanks.

Anytime we stopped the bus to take pictures, or to get out for any reason, and it seemed we were stopping all the time, we were covered with mosquitoes. They even boarded the bus while we were outside, and sat waiting for us to return (none of them had tickets). I had always thought things were big down in Texas, but Alaskan mosquitoes take the prize. I think Alaska should call them the state bird.

As a joke, I have often told people that I had to take the dogs off the side of the bus at night and bring them into my room because they were crying so much from the bites of the large mosquitoes.

We had to go through a check station on entering Alaska, but it was no big deal because I was asked if we had any plants and so forth and they always took my word for it when I said no.

I did have to buy a pro-rated license plate for the bus while in Alaska, which I was not prepared to deal with. There was nothing mentioned about the plate in my charter papers, and there was no money for it in the "Alaska Kit." Rather than call Greyhound on a pay phone, I came up with the seventy-five dollar fee out of my own money and got out of jail so to speak. We were free to go now, and we continued on to Fairbanks.

On arriving in Fairbanks, we were welcomed by the heat wave that was prevailing at the time. The temperature was up to 97 degrees and there was no air-conditioning in any of the hotels or motels. It was very uncomfortable for a couple days.

We took a boat cruise down the Tanana River and saw where gold was discovered at the mouth of Cripple Creek where it enters the Tanana. On down the river we stopped at an Island and visited an authentic replica of a native Eskimo home. We were shown how they stored their food in storage sheds that were built high off the ground to keep animals from getting into it. We also watched their fish wheels in action and saw the way they cleaned and dried the salmon they caught. There were sheds full of hanging dried fish to be used for their own use through the winter months and also to feed their dogs. A student, of Eskimo decent, was our narrator while on the Island. After explaining how and why they did certain things, she would end her story by adding,

"Now ain't that sumthin?"

This is a phrase that I have never forgotten and I find myself using the same words quite often.

"Now ain't that sumthin?"

There might have been a few people in the group that were in the eighties but you would never have known it by watching them. Every time we stopped the bus or when the boat pulled into shore, everyone would get off and explore and enjoy the stop to the fullest. I really think everyone got his or her moneys worth out of this trip.

Our Narrator

Mouth of Cripple Creek

After four days in Fairbanks we were ready to board the Alaska Railway and go to McKinley National Park. I think it is now known as Denali National Park.

Our bus on flatcar at rear of train

I was told to have my bus at the depot an hour before the train was scheduled to depart so I had to get the group up and out early that morning. At the rail yard they had me drive the bus onto a flatcar, which was then coupled onto the last car of the train. The bus went along as "excess baggage," and it only cost me eighteen dollars. What a bargain! There again there were no provisions for that charge in the, "Alaska Kit." My group got off at the Mt. McKinley Park Lodge, but I had to continue on to Anchorage to take the bus off the flatcar, It seemed they were short of flatcars and there was a need for me to get it off as soon as we arrived in Anchorage.

While still aboard the train, I talked and visited with the conductors and I asked them where they stayed, while in Anchorage. I was told to go to a certain hotel and tell Betty to give me a dark room. I have forgotten the hotel's name.

I also learned how accommodating the railroad could be for people living there, or for any passenger as far as that goes. An individual could ride the train out to any place of his choosing along the track, and be let off. When you finished your hike, or when and if you killed an elk, you could drag it to the railroad and the train would stop anywhere along the track, to pick up you and your elk.

I arrived in Anchorage two days before my group was scheduled to arrive, so I spent my time sleeping. I am the type that needs darkness to be able to sleep and I had been deprived of that darkness for the last week.

On arrival in Anchorage, I unloaded my bus from the flat car and went directly to the hotel. I walked up to the counter and asked the lady if she might be Betty. She said she was and asked how she could help me. I told her the conductors on the train had recommended I stay there and for her to give me a dark room. She had me sign in and gave me a key with the number 205 on it. I assumed I was to be on the second floor, but from the outside, the building appeared to be a single story. I turned and asked where the stairway was. She said to take the stairs going down. What a surprise! When I got down to my room and turned off the lights, I have never seen such darkness. The ventilation system was tremendous and it was blowing in cool fresh air.

I finally awakened with severe hunger pains and after going upstairs and inquiring whether it was day or night. I found I had slept from four PM the day before until eleven-thirty, that morning. I had finally caught up on my sleep. Now it was only a matter of time before I would be picking up my group, so we could be one big happy family again.

"Now ain't that sumthin?"

They had just started building the new highway to connect Fair-banks with Anchorage. It was to be opened for travel in the summer of 1972. However, at that time, the Alaska railroad was the only connection between the two Cities.

In Fairbanks it was hot and the sun never seemed to go down. There was just too much daylight for me and I was dying for a good nights sleep. In Anchorage I had darkness and it was very cool which made it nice for sleeping.

I met the train and was greeted by everyone. It seemed they had really missed me and were anxious to get back to their bus.

The next day we took a drive down to Seward to see some of the damage done by the earthquake that had happened only a few years earlier. We saw our first glacier on our way back from Seward and pulled into the parking lot to get a close-up look at a real glacier. It was very cold and it did not take the group very long to see and admire the glacier and to start boarding the bus again.

I think that stop was the only one we made, while in Alaska, that we were not eaten up by mosquitoes when we were outside the bus.

We only stayed in Anchorage a couple of days before it was time to reverse our northwest trek and head back in a southerly direction.

We took the road to Tok Junction again, as we were going back to Whitehorse. I was to leave my group in Whitehorse and deadhead the bus back to Tok, and then over to Haines, where I would await their arrival the next day. The group would then be taking the narrow gauge railroad over the mountain to Skagway.

This railroad transported many gold seekers traveling over the mountain to reach the gold fields. Many went by train but hundreds took to the well-worn trails on foot during the peak of the gold rush days. This was the shortest way to the gold fields and there was an urgency to get there as quickly as possible. Many died from the cold while others died of sickness and injuries. Everyone had his own dream of becoming a wealthy individual overnight. Lots of these men lost their lives before ever reaching the gold fields.

Beaver Pond

On the trip to Haines, I had all day to spend by myself with no rush to get there. I stopped and took lots of pictures. I spent over an hour just exploring a beaver pond. The beavers had cut lots of small birch trees and used the trunks for building their dam and the small tender limbs they used for food. I spent lots of time just walking around the pond, which was quite large. The water in the pond was extremely clear and I could see the bottom. I waited very quietly and patiently for a while but never saw any beavers. I am sure there was a family living there as some of the birch trees were freshly cut. Maybe the sentry on duty warned of my approach and the others took the warning seriously. Anyway I never saw any beavers. I did pick up a piece of a birch log that had been cut on both ends by their sharp teeth. It was about two feet long and eight inches in diameter and I put it in the baggage bin and brought it home to put in my garden.

It was a very pleasant trip just meandering along, knowing I had the whole day to goof off. I stopped many times to admire the beauty of the snow- capped mountains. I traveled through an area along the road where I could see how the earth was made up. I could only see a couple of inches of topsoil on top of the rocks and I could easily understand why the trees would not grow to any size. However, with only two inches of soil, there seemed to be no lack of growth anywhere.

I finally arrived in Haines and found it was definitely not a tourist town. There was nothing there but a few stores. I went over to the old Ft. Chilikoot Barracks and found a room for the night in one of the old houses that used to be one of the Commanding Officer's houses, during the time the Ft. was active. There were two of these old houses left and they were in immaculate condition. Someone had seen the possibilities in making each of these two buildings into a six room Bed and Breakfast. There was a huge dining room, large enough to seat all guests, and they served all the meals family style. That night I enjoyed the most delicious baked salmon dinner I have ever eaten. I hated to leave the place the next morning, especially after having a lumberjack breakfast of ham and eggs with fresh homemade biscuits and gravy, but I said goodbye and drove my bus to the dock in Haines.

There were close to two hundred acres of parade grounds adjacent to the two large houses. These homes were surrounded by a huge well kept lawn that was beautifully landscaped with trees and shrubbery.

This fort was built in 1902 and was used very little except for the many parades and for the perfecting of the soldiers shooting skills. At one time there were as many as four hundred soldiers stationed there. The soldiers had little to do except maintain the lawns and gardens themselves. When the Army no longer had any use for the Fort, it was closed permanently in 1947.

The ship coming in to Haines

I could see the ship tied up at the dock across the bay at Skagway. Soon the ship had left Skagway and was now crossing the bay to pick up the rest of the passengers waiting at the dock in Haines. I had driven the bus into the line of vehicles waiting for the ship to arrive. When the ship was securely tied up to the dock, the loading ramp was lowered and the vehicles started coming aboard. There are twenty to twenty-five vehicles of different breeds that go aboard, some vehicles with trailers, a few trucks and lots of cars. The ramp was then raised and we got under way, immediately.

For the next three days, I was free to sit on the deck with my binoculars and watch the whales along side the ship. There were hundreds of bald eagles sitting in trees all along the shoreline. What a hard life a Greyhound driver sometimes had to endure, but someone had to do it.

Now ain't that sumthin?

We enjoyed the slow relaxing trip through the Inland Passage, visiting Juneau, Sitka, and Wrangell. We were taken through some areas where icebergs were plentiful. The Captain took the ship, slowly, into the icebergs for some close-up photography and then slowly backed out. Some of the icebergs were small but a few were quite large. The portion that you see above water is very small compared to the amount you can't see below the surface.

Arriving in Juneau

We pulled into Juneau and the ship tied up for an hour. Everyone got off and walked through the town. Since it is the Capital of Alaska we wanted to say we had been there. Everyone enjoyed the stroll through town and getting to peek into the "Bucket of Blood" tavern and other historical places that we had read about. There was a paved street going out of town in both directions but the road ended a short ways out. Actually I don't remember seeing any cars parked on the street.

The portion of our sea journey ended and I drove the bus off the ship when we arrived in Prince Rupert. We then took to the highway and spent our first night in Smithers, B.C. I never gave Smithers much thought but since I was there in 1971, I have flown back into Smithers twice, to go steelhead fishing on the Babine River, about 125 miles north. We were flown into this lodge by bush plane and I must say it was an experience. I was in a group with six fellows from Stockton that had gone on a fishing trip for a week, fishing on the Babine.

Our next night, was spent in Prince George at the same motel we had used on our way up to Dawson Creek. After leaving Prince George, we were pretty much traveling the same route that we used coming up from Kamloops. The rest of the trip was uneventful as we were just covering miles to take us home.

On July 11, we arrived back in Lodi, and I unloaded the baggage for the final time.

At the end of these trips, there was always a big let down. You had grown to know each one personally, and you were accustomed to seeing everyone every day and being able to talk about things we had seen along our way. Now there was the feeling of losing the family you had come to know and love so much. There would no longer be the roll calls in the mornings, telling that little private joke before boarding the bus, getting everyone aboard the bus, and no longer having another exciting day to look forward to with the group, wondering where we were going to have our coffee break that morning.

But in this case, I lived in Lodi, and I was always running into lots of the group daily, so my leaving at this time was not all that bad. There would be lots more charters with the Lodi Travel Club, as they usually took at least three of these trips each year.

WOW!   Can you imagine?   I really got to drive the Alaska Highway.

Now ain't that sumthin?

Chapter 8

CANADA AND THE CANADIAN ROCKIES

In June 1966, I took the Lodi Travel Club on a three-week trip through Canada. We drove up the Coast Highway to Vancouver to start our trip. The next day we began our journey across the Trans-Canada Highway Number 1. We drove to the little town of Hope, BC for our first overnight stop. The next morning we took a side trip on the Hope-Princeton highway to the area of the big slide that happened in the early morning hours of January 9, 1965.

For about a mile, it seemed half the mountain had slid off and covered the highway running through the narrow valley. The slide had filled the valley with rock and dirt and had the highway blocked for through traffic between Hope and Princeton. The slide came off the mountain from the north side of the road and slid down across the valley and up the other side like spilled water, wiping out all the trees in its path. It then came back across the valley, finally seeking a level in the bottom of the valley. It had covered the valley floor to a depth of 250 to 300 feet. This was the largest slide in Canadian History. After surveying the damage to the highway, it was decided the only solution would be to build a new highway up and over the slide. There was just too much rock and earth to be removed in order to get down to the old highway. There were four people who lost their lives to the slide while driving along the highway that early morning, being covered by tons of debris. We drove across the slide, then turned around and went back to Hope. If you are ever traveling the Trans-Canada Highway and go through the little city of Hope, It is definitely worth your time to take a detour at Hope and see this phenomenon.

We were now headed in a North East direction on the Trans-Canada Highway. We followed the Frazer River for quite a ways. It provided us with spectacular views around each corner. A large volume of melting glacier water flows down this river and it is a yellowish brown in color. This color was caused, by the grinding of rocks, as the Glacier slid down the side of the mountain. The River is not accessible in most places, as the banks are cut deep in solid rock. It was a very beautiful drive, with the Canadian Pacific Railroad traversing the other side of the river and going through numerous tunnels and over bridges. We spent lots of time stopping and reading historical signs along the road telling how the road was built and all of the problems the construction crews encountered while building it.

The Mighty Frazier River

The winters were harsh and work was very slow due to the snow and the extreme cold temperatures they had to endure.

Mile after mile we watched the muddy Frazer River flow along side the Highway. The scenery was rugged and beautiful.

We arrived in Revelstoke and spent a pleasant night there. When we arrived, we could see a forest fire burning on the mountain behind our motel. I watched plane after plane dropping fire retardant on the flames and in no time it seemed, the fire was extinguished. On leaving Revelstoke, we started climbing and were immediately surrounded with beautiful large pine trees.

Rest stop atop Rogers Pass

We drove through several long tunnels, which were actually snow sheds, to protect the Highway from snow slides in the winter. We came to a rest area at the top of Rogers Pass. Here we stopped for a while and everyone got out to take pictures and enjoy the scenery. It was so peaceful, just sitting there, taking in the beauty of the mountains and the snow. I think the Rogers Pass area is one of my favorite spots along the Trans-Canada Highway and as many times as I have been there, I will never cease to revel in its beauty.

We had lunch in Golden and from there we were not too far from Lake Louise, our next over night stop. Lake Louise has a beautiful old stone hotel built by the Canadian Railroad in 1890. A fire destroyed most of the Chalet a few years later and the hotel, as it is now, was finished in 1925. At that time the name was changed to Chateau Lake Louise

There is a small lake in the front of the hotel that is surrounded by high mountains, and there's a glacier in the background.

Lake Louise

You can hike around the lake on a smooth trail and it offers spectacular views, looking back at the hotel. You could spend a few hours exploring the hotel and the many gardens surrounding it. I do not think there is a prettier sight than sitting on the front porch of the hotel, gazing at the glacier at the end of Lake Louise. We spent two days there, as there were several interesting places to visit within a half hours drive.

The Hotel still used the old English style of paging for it's guest and the Bell Capitan runs through the hotel crying out, "Telephone call for Mr. Jones, calling for Mr. Jones."

It reminded me of the old Phillip Morris commercial.

Chateau Lake Louise

Staying at the hotel truly gives you the feeling of elegance experienced by the upper English Class. I almost felt out of place while staying there.

The next morning we drove south of Lake Louise to the beautiful and peaceful Moraine Lake. We enjoyed the mirror smooth water. It too had a glacier sitting at the head of the lake. It is known for its serenity and smooth waters. The water in the lakes of Canada, are the bluest of blue, or else they are milky.

We left Lake Louise and headed North to Jasper. It is around a hundred miles but you were in for some of the most gorgeous views you will ever see in the Canadian Rockies. There are several large glaciers on the way and many beautiful lakes.

Columbia Ice Fields

About halfway to Jasper we came to the Columbia Ice Fields. You can see the foot of the Glacier up close from the Highway without leaving the bus. We drove up the left side of the Glacier with the bus, and I had to use the lowest gear to pull the steep hill. There is a Visitors Center halfway up the side of the Glacier. There you can take the snow cat for a ride out on the glacier.

The Visitor's Center was as far as I could take the bus. All the passengers got out and walked out onto the ice field. It was very cold and we did not stay out of the snow cat very long. The driver stopped the vehicle over a large crevice, so we could take a look down into the depths of the ice. This crevice was two feet across and as far as you could see down into the ice, it was a beautiful bluish green color. The ice is two to three hundred feet deep. However, since the first time I visited the glacier, it has been receding at an alarming rate.

Mountain on road to Jasper

Greyhound owned the concession at the Columbia Ice Fields when we were there, but the Brewster Transportation

Company out of Banff operated the tour buses. In 1965 Brewster sold all of its operations to Greyhound. But since that time I am told Brewster has attained all of the property again. I think this happened about the same time Laidlaw bought the Greyhound Cooperation. The tour bus business between Banff and Jasper is a lucrative business and there were lots of Brewster buses on the road serving all points of interest.

The Ice Fields are so popular because you can pull into the parking area, at the foot of the Glacier, and easily walk out on it. How far you want to walk depends on you. There are trails onto the ice and you can go as far as you like. The Columbia Ice Fields have the largest accumulation of snow and ice south of the Arctic Circle. The Ice Fields are located on the Continental Divide, with melting waters flowing into the Arctic, Pacific and the Atlantic Oceans.

The Athabasca Glacier is the largest of the glaciers. This Glacier is awesome, and to stand at the foot of it and think how many hundreds of years some of the ice has been there, makes ones life seem so insignificant. The first time I saw the glacier, the foot of it was much closer to the road. On return trips it seems to have melted a lot.

We left the Ice Fields and continued north to Jasper. We spent two days there as there was much to see in the Jasper National Park and Jasper sits right in the middle of it. Maligne Lake is probably the most visited attraction located there but I enjoyed the ride on the Jasper Tramway most of all. This tram is the longest aerial tramway to be found anywhere in Canada. It will take you up 8,200 feet to a peak on the mountain overlooking Jasper. What a view you have looking out over the valley below. You can see for miles and there are several lakes, from that vantage point, to be seen.

The Athabasca Falls is another beautiful place that we enjoyed very much. The Athabasca River runs through a narrow funneled area that has cut through quartz-rich sandstone rock and has created a deep gorge that leaves you in awe when you look down into it.

We left Jasper and headed back the way we had come, on our way to the quaint little town of Banff. The first time I visited Banff, the stores were full of Canadian woolen clothing. Now the Japanese have taken over and there is a mixture of everything found there.

We took a tram ride to the top of a mountain south of town, which gave us a fabulous view. The famous, Banff Springs Hotel, was also built by the Canadian Pacific Railroad, and it rivals the Chateau Lake Louise. We drove by the hotel golf course and saw several herds of elk feeding and laying on the fairways. I don't know what happens when golfers approach.

Quaint little town of Banff

View from tram behind Banff-Bow River

Maybe the elk are polite enough to clear the fairway and let them play through. The Bow River is beautiful as it meanders behind the Banff Springs Hotel.

After a couple of days in Banff, we moved on to Calgary. This is where the World Championship Rodeo is held each fall. We were a little early for this event but we did see the rodeo grounds where it is held.

We spent one night in Calgary and headed south to the Waterton Lakes hotel. This hotel, the Prince of Wales, is a little off the beaten path but it is another one of the hotels built by the Canadian Pacific Railroad in beautiful, selected spots. It sits all by it's self on a little knoll by the shores of beautiful Waterton Lake, with no trees around it. It does have Waterton Lake sitting behind it to give it some glamour or it would be a mighty drab looking place. It is not one of my favorite places to visit.

We spent the night there and found it to be a very cold unfriendly place, as the wind came whistling down from the snow-laden mountains and across the lake. The next morning we left Waterton Lakes and went south to Glacier National Park in Montana.

The Park Service would not allow me to transport my people through the park in my bus. My instruction from Greyhound was to leave my passengers at the East Entrance and deadhead the bus around the southern part of the park, which would be about one hundred miles further. The Park Service would then take my passengers in their buses and go thru the park. I would then pick them up at the West Entrance. I happened to mention to one of the Rangers that I should get started, as the trip around the park would take lots of time.

He said, "Why don't you take your bus through the park it is much shorter. You can take it through empty, we just don't want you transporting your passengers through as we need the extra revenue for the Park."

I suppose they would lose lots of revenue if they did not operate that way. I know I sure appreciated them letting me drive my bus through the Park, as I had never been there and I had plenty of time to stop and take pictures. Even with me taking my time going through the Park I still arrived at our hotel an hour before my group got there.

The drive through the park was beautiful. I left ahead of my group and was able to stop often and take pictures at points of interest. Since we were staying at the lodge at the west entrance, and I had arrived quite sometime before my group, I unloaded the baggage and had it into their room before they even got there. I had time to settle in and relax a bit before they arrived.

The next morning we started for home. We went to Kalispell and then followed the Flat Head Lake to Missoula. From Missoula we drove to Idaho Falls, then into Nevada and west to Reno. After a night in Reno we were all ready to get home.

St. Mary's Lake near east entrance

Once again we had a marvelous trip and one to remember for a long time. I look at my pictures of these trips I have taken, and I can relive every one of them. The pictures are a constant reminder to me, of how fortunate I have been, and how right I was, when I made my decision to become a Greyhound Bus Driver.

It has been a good life, and, some one had to do it.

Chapter 9

CUSTER'S BATTLEFIELD

My life as a Greyhound bus driver got more exciting as time went on. I never knew where I would be going, or what I would be doing until I was called to work each day. We had five schedules going to Harrah's Club, and three going to other clubs at the lake, on a daily basis. The morning schedules usually over-loaded, and there would be one to two extra sections added to take care of all the passengers. I had just returned to the Stockton depot one evening, after finishing one of these trips. I signed in and the dispatcher said,

"Morgan, you have a charter out of Sonora with the Sonora High School the twenty first of June, do you want to take it?"

I took the charter papers and looked them over. I had been requested to drive the High School, Indian Enrichment Class, to the Little Big Horn in Wyoming. This trip was to coincide with the one hundredth anniversary of Custer's Last Stand. I did not recognize the name on the charter paper but I figured I had been recommended by someone who new me so I would honor the request.

"Yes, I will take it." I replied.

I had never been in this area before and it should be an interesting trip, however, I never enjoyed driving school kids too much because most of their trips were very noisy. I did want to see Custer's battlefield though, and that was the reason for making the decision to go.

On June 21, I left Stockton for Sonora, which lies about sixty-five miles to the east, in the foothills of the Sierra Nevada Mountains. As I pulled the bus into the school parking lot, there were lots of kids and parents waiting for me. The parents wanted to see that their kid got away safely. There was a stack of tents, sleeping bags, stoves and cooking utensils. For once I was told to stand back and let the kids load everything. They needed to know just where each item was stored. Hey, I am beginning to like these kids already and they are not even on the bus. After everything was loaded and the kids were aboard, the teacher said we were ready to roll.

We departed Sonora for the celebration of the hundredth anniversary of the Battle of the Little Big Horn. The teacher told me he had requested me as their driver, on the advice of a friend, who had gone on several charter trips with me before. I told him I appreciated the opportunity to be driving for him on this trip and would try to live up to his friend's trust in me.

I was given a copy of the itinerary and it looked very good. Each night we would be stopping and camping in roadside rest areas along the high way. The teacher had a letter from the State Highway Department authorizing the use of such stops. I would never have guessed the Highway Dept. would have allowed it, but we had their approval in black and white and that was all we needed.

We stopped just before we got to Lovelock, Nevada, pulling into a nice rest area. There were picnic tables, water fountains and rest rooms. What more could you ask for when you are camping out. It had almost, all the comforts of home. The kids began unloading what they needed, and in pre-assigned groups, they started putting up tents and setting up cooking facilities. These different work groups were assigned their duties before starting on the trip and they were responsible for that job for the entire trip. There were cleanup crews to clean the area before we left each site in the mornings. I ate a few meals with the kids, but most of the time I took the bus and went into the nearest town in search of a motel. My bones did not appreciate the hard ground and discomfort of a sleeping bag, plus I needed a shower each day. After getting the kids unloaded and settled I would usually drive to the closest town and have my dinner at a restaurant. I would always have breakfast before driving back the next morning.

We worked our way along thru central Nevada and turned left at Wells. Going north into Idaho, we crossed into Wyoming and entered West Yellowstone. We continued until we came to the main campgrounds where our cabins awaited. It was pre-arranged for the kids to sleep in cabins, bunked four to the cabin, so they got a break from sleeping on the ground. However they did cook their own meals while in Yellowstone. These kids averaged about sixteen or seventeen years in age and we had three chaperons along to help keep them in line, however from my observations, they needed very little help as they were a bunch of good kids.

One of the boys had a telescoping rod and reel and a couple of fishing lures that he had brought along. He decided he was going to catch some trout for their dinner. He asked if I wanted to go along, so being the fisherman I am, I went along to watch. We walked around behind the cabins and down to the river. On his first cast he caught a rainbow, about three pounds. On his next cast, another fish! Cast after cast resulted in catches each time, until he had about twenty-five fish spilling over from a washtub. I said, "Hey guys, lets stop this, you have more than enough fish."

As far as I know, there is no fishing allowed in the camp ground at all, and that was the reason so many fish were caught.

One of the boys said, "We are part Indian, we can fish anywhere and catch all we want."

Which I am not sure is true. I suppose they figured they had plenty (which they did), so they cleaned them there by the river and took the fish to the cook, and we had fresh trout for dinner that night. I ate with them, and I must say it was a very tasty meal, to be prepared by novice cooks. All these kids were of Indian Ancestry and this venture was for credit in their history class.

One of the boys was very sick with leukemia before we left and his folks did not want him to go. His doctor had given permission for the boy to go on this trip, saying he had such a short time to be around, he might as well enjoy every minute. He had been looking forward, with such anticipation, to going with his class that his folks decided to give in to his wishes. At least if something happened he would die happy, doing what he wanted most, being with his friends.

I did not know the extent of his illness when we began our trip. I did know we had an oxygen bottle aboard when we started, but for what use, I did not know. When we left Yellowstone, we took Highway 212 for Billings, Montana. We had to cross a range of mountains almost 11,000 feet high. As we came to the summit, there was lots of snow along the roadside and the kids asked their teacher if we could stop so they could play in it. We did stop, and almost everyone got off the bus, except for a couple of kids. We had only been there a few minutes, when one of the kids came off the bus and told the teacher that, (I have forgotten his name so I will call him John for now) John had passed out and was not breathing.

We loaded as quickly as possible and began a fast trip down the mountain. In the meantime, the oxygen came into play. They got John to breathing again but he did not look good at all. Luckily, at the bottom of the mountain, we came to the town of Red Lodge, and a hospital sign directed us to the emergency room. Thankfully, there was a Doctor on duty and he saw John immediately. We spent about two hours waiting before they had John stabilized, and the Doctor said he must remain there at the Hospital.

This little incident put a hush and a feeling of sadness over the entire bus. All the kids were very fond of John and were deeply saddened to know he had put up such a gallant effort, to no avail, in trying to stay healthy enough to make this trip.

John remained at the Red Lodge Hospital for five days and his folks decided to drive up in their car to take him home. He could not be flown by private aircraft because of the high altitude that would be encountered by flying through the mountains.

We spent the night in a rest area near Billings, and it was indeed, a very sad and quiet night. The next day, we pulled up to the Visitor's Center, at Custer's Battlefield.

It was June 25th, 1976, just one hundred years ago to the day, since the battle that left no white man standing or living, happened on this very spot. Chills went up my spine. I stood up in front of the bus and said,

"Kids, this is the place where Custer got the shit kicked out of him."

I received an instant roar of applause, and I knew I had expressed the feeling being held by each one of them.

My thoughts and feelings toward General Custer were always negative. I truly believe his arrogance, in trying to be a hero, brought him to his own demise. He had it coming but I do feel sorrow for all the men under his command.

From the top of the hill Custer and his men could oversee the Little Big Horn and the men had moved over the hill to the sunny side and were lying in the grass. Little did they know, at this very minute, the Indians were leaving the Little Big Horn, under cover of trees, through a ravine on Custer's right side. Custer and his men were unaware of this movement. In a very short time the Indians came in hordes, over the hill behind them and had them surrounded. The battle was a complete surprise for Custer and his men as they thought the Indians were still down on the river.

Custer's Battleground—Little Big Horn in distance

While sitting on the hillside, looking at all the little white crosses, I had an eerie sense of what Custer might have felt, when he looked back and saw the hundreds of warriors coming over the hill behind him. With no chance for help, he knew he had pushed too far and had made a terrible mistake. He knew this time he had made the biggest blunder of his career in his quest for fame and glory.

My eyes wandered across the rolling hillside and saw places where there was only a single cross. Then there would be two crosses standing all by themselves in a little ravine. Some single crosses could be seen as far as two hundred yards away.

I visualized these men trying desperately to reach safety, only to be run down by hordes of Indians. I could imagine these individuals running for dear life, only to be brought down by the overpowering blow of a tomahawk or an arrow.

There was a group of many crosses near the top of the hill. This spot is where the soldiers made a combined effort to hold off the Indians, but the shear number was just too great and every single soldier met a horrible death on that day.

We boarded the bus again and drove east on a gravel road, about five or six miles and turned into a pasture where there were lots of authentic Indian Tee-Pees already set up. Indians had come from all over the world to celebrate this great event, the one hundredth anniversary of the Battle with Custer. My group was to pitch their tents in the pasture among all the others, and spend the next two days and nights in celebration with those camped there. The property used for this celebration belonged to the grandson of Chief Two-Moons. The Chief had fought in the battle defeating Custer. The grandson came out to the bus when we pulled up to his house. I was introduced to him and he showed us where to pitch the tents.

The grandson invited me to stay and sleep in his house while we were there, but I declined, making some legitimate excuse. I had been very observant on driving into the pasture that day, and the Indians did not look at me with too much love and friendship in their hearts. Could it be they were still pissed at the white man? Or were they just curious on seeing a Greyhound bus there in the pasture. Maybe an Indian just has that unfriendly look about him all time --- maybe it is just his natural look.

I figured there was no need for me to find out, or take a chance, so the safest place for me that night would be to light a shuck and get out of there before nightfall So I dead-headed my bus back into Billings, (the nearest motel) and since the bus was needed the next day, I had to dead-head back to the ranch (175 miles round-trip). Since I was not paying for the fuel and I was not charging the miles to the Charter, I did not worry too much about the mileage.

The celebrations were held at night so I didn't get to see any of them. The kids enjoyed the celebration very much and from the reports they gave me they participated in the ceremonial dancing.

After the second day the celebration ended and everyone started taking their tents down and getting packed up to leave. I pulled the bus into the pasture one last time, and a tired, weary bunch of kids loaded their gear, saying a goodbye to their new found friends and we left for home.

We took a little different route coming home, since the excitement of the camping and the gathering at the Two-Moons ranch was over, they wanted to get home as soon as possible. That was fine with me because this trip had worn me out also.

On our arrival in Sonora, all the parents were waiting to pick up their kids and a lot of classmates had gathered to welcome them home also. It seemed they could not wait until the next day to find out all about the trip. The weather had also changed since we had left and it had become much hotter. After everything was unloaded from the bus, I went back inside to make sure no one had left anything behind, and finding nothing, I stepped back outside the bus and was thanking the teacher and the chaperones for making my trip enjoyable when someone said,

"Grady, we have a little gift for you."

With that, one of the girls stepped up on the first step of the bus and said, "The Sonora High School Indian Enrichment Class would like to thank you for the wonderful trip you have given us. We obtained this gourd that was used in the ceremonial dance, of the one-hundredth anniversary of the Battle of the Little Big Horn, with George Armstrong Custer. We would like to present it to you in appreciation for your being so helpful throughout our trip and making it so enjoyable."

This brought tears to my eyes as they had completely caught me off guard. I had no idea they had done this, as I was not at the celebration. It was a well kept secret all the way home. I opened the box that they had wrapped so beautifully, and attached to the gourd, was a little card that read:

"This gourd is presented to Grady Morgan to show our appreciation to him for going out of his way to make our trip an enjoyable one. This gourd was used in the Indian Gourd Dance at the Celebration on the Two-Moons ranch, on June 25th, 1976."

Signed: The Sonora High School Indian Enrichment Program.

What a wonderful way to end a beautiful trip, having had the chance to live with and better understand the actions of this younger generation up close.

I cherished the opportunity to sit on the hillside where the battle took place and try to absorb the feelings that Custer must have felt in his dying moments, I kept coming up with this thought,

"My God, where did all these Indians come from? I should have paid more attention to the warnings I received."

I have read about the Battle of the Little Big Horn all my life and it has always seemed so far away in time that I had given it little thought until I visited the site one hundred years to the day after it happened.

Now I realize it happened only a lifetime ago.

Chapter 10

A TRIP TO DEATH VALLEY

The Lodi Travel Club had planned a trip into Death Valley for a week and then over to Las Vegas for another week of gambling and sighting seeing. We started the trip on a beautiful day the sixteenth of April and it looked as if we would be blessed with nice weather for the entire trip. The best time to visit Death Valley is no later than early spring, otherwise it would be to hot. We stayed at the motel in Stove Pipe Wells. This location seemed to be centrally located in order to visit all the points of interest in Death Valley.

Lady Bird Johnson and me

While we were having dinner the first night, I could see into the room next to ours and there sat Lady Bird Johnson in the dining room. Being the out going person that I am, I walked in and asked if I might get a picture with her. She seemed happy to do so and stood up and shook hands with me.

She was there checking with the National Parks as she was the chair-person for all the National Parks at the time Lyndon Johnson was president.

The first day we went to the northern end of the valley to the Ubehebe Crater. This is an extinct volcano from years ago. It is shaped like a cone sunken into the ground, instead of the usual mountain of lava. After seeing the crater we drove to Scotty's Castle.

An old prospector by the name of Scotty built this Castle. It takes a couple of hours to go through the Castle and is a very interesting place to see. Scotty was said to have found a gold mine in the valley, but a Mr. Johnson from back east, financed the building of the Castle and he spent considerable time there after it was finished. His health was failing fast and his doctor advised a drier climate. This was the reason he chose Death Valley. He felt so much better while he was there. Everyone thinks the gold mine that Scotty had found was Mr. Johnson. Never the less, Scotty's friendship was a tremendous help to Mr. Johnson and vise versa. Scotty never lived in the Castle, but preferred to live in a shack a couple of miles down the road, at the foot of the hill. After visiting the Castle and going up on the hill behind the Castle to see Scotties gravesite, we started back to the motel.

The next day we went to the southern end of the valley to Bad Water. This spot is 282 ft. below sea level and the lowest point in the Western Hemisphere. The temperature in the valley is the hottest in the U.S. They hauled Borax out of the valley with the famed, "Twenty Mule Team." Death valley is full of rugged beauty and yet is very pleasant if you are there in the early spring, but do not go in the summer time for your own comfort.

We took some interesting side trips on our way back to the motel. There are lots of things to see all over the southern end of the valley.

The next day, before leaving for Las Vegas, we had lunch at the Death Valley Inn. We had just gotten into the restaurant and I was seated next to the Tour Director when the waitress came to our table and ask if I was the bus driver for the group.

I said, "Yes."

She said, "You have a phone call Sir."

I thought surely the call is for not for me, but I did not see any other bus in the parking lot so I followed her to the phone and picked it up. When I answered it I was not ready for the message I was about to receive.

It was my ex-wife and she held back no words in giving me her message. "Kenneth was killed this morning."

Kenneth was my only son.

After getting a few details of what had happened I thanked her for calling to let me know and hung up. It was as if she had called to tell me a business deal had fallen through. The words did not sink in. I walked back to the table and sat down. I must have looked terrible because the Tour Conductor asked me what was wrong. I said, "My son was killed this morning."

Then the shock of what I had just said, hit me like a ton of bricks! I started crying, uncontrollably, and I asked to be excused from the table. I walked out onto the Patio and sat down. "Could I have prevented this, had I been there?"

All of a sudden it seemed my fault that this had happened because I was not there to protect him and I began weeping again. I had tried to teach safety to my son when he was growing up but I felt, now, that I had failed, miserably.

The Tour Conductor came out and sat with me and held my hand. She asked if Greyhound could send another driver to take them on to Las Vegas. I said, "They will, if I call, but I am not going to. I am driving you folks on to Las Vegas myself." She was concerned, and had every right to be, that I was not up to driving safely. But I had already given thought to this situation and had come to the conclusion that it would be much faster for me to drive to Las Vegas than to wait on a relief driver.

When Greyhound calls a driver in to work, they have to give him an hour and a half notice. Then by the time he gets out to me three or four hours will have passed. We then have a bus sitting there in Death Valley and another driver will have to be sent out to bring it in. I could be there in two hours and I could solve this problem very easily. I was going to get us there safely. I was in full control of my self and I need to get to Las Vegas, for I would be flying home. Let's load the bus and be off. I kept myself under control all the way and everyone seemed to relax after we got started.

When we arrived at our hotel in Las Vegas, I pulled the bus into the unloading area. The Bell Captain came out of the hotel and walked directly to me. He said, "Mr. Morgan, was your wife able to get in touch with you this morning?"

I said, "Yes she was, thank you."

He replied, "We are very sorry to hear about your son, and for your convenience, we have a limousine waiting to take you to the airport. We also took the liberty of checking with the Airlines and we have your flight booked. We thought you would be wanting to get home as quickly as possible."

He said the flight was to leave in five minutes, but for me not to worry, they did fortunately, have a little clout with the airlines and they would hold my flight until I arrived.

I told him that I would need to take the bus to the Dispatchers Office, after it was unloaded, in order to leave the charter papers and the bus, before I could go to the airport, so the limousine followed me. After dropping the bus at the Dispatch Office, we made it to the airport in record time. We were about twenty minutes late. I started for the ticket counter and one of the clerks came running up to me and said,

"Your ticket is already taken care of and they are waiting for you to board the plane, Sir." She took me to the plane and I walked onboard.

No one paid any attention to me when I boarded and I wonder if they had been told why the delay or maybe they were used to the airlines always being late. Once settled in my seat, I began sobbing again. I was shedding tears for my son and for the thoughtfulness of this Club in helping me when the chips were down.

My feelings for these large Gambling Casinos changed that day. I had always thought of them as being heartless, and out to get your money. I had heard stories of people losing all their money, and the Clubs providing them bus fare to get home, but I had never actually seen it.

A couple of weeks after I got home and got myself back together, I wrote the management of this Casino to express my sincere appreciation for what they did for me that day. I would like to acknowledge the Casino by name, but I have visited too many Casinos since this happened and it was too long ago for me to remember. I can truthfully say that the management of these Casinos are real people and do have a heart, they are ready to help anyone in time of need, and I will forever be grateful to them.

When my son was killed, my ex-wife felt she had a moral responsibility to track me down and notify me herself, instead of letting Greyhound do it. She had called the Greyhound Dispatcher in Stockton and asked if they might know where I could be contacted. After explaining the need to contact me, they had given her a copy of my itinerary. She then called the Casino in Las Vegas where we would be staying that night and started back tracking my schedule until she found me in the Death Valley Inn.

My son was in the U.S. Navy and had just turned twenty-one. He was in the prime of his life, with so much to give and live for. God must have had a very important place for him in Heaven and it is not for me to ask why. I have missed him terribly but the knowledge of knowing he was a Christian has kept me going.

Kenneth had just served a six-month tour in the South Pacific and had returned with his ship to Port Chicago, where they were unloading ammunition.

While in Japan, Kenneth had bought a new M. G. Sports car and had it shipped back to California on an aircraft carrier. A couple of weeks after he came home, his car arrived and he went to San Francisco to pick it up. He had driven over to visit his mother for the weekend and on his way back to the ship on Monday morning, he had his fatal accident.

Being a bus driver and knowing the value of safety, and having attended lots of safety seminars, I thought I had conveyed all the rules of safe driving to my son.

I felt I had failed, miserably.

Kenneth Lynn Morgan---Age 21

Chapter 11

OTHER CHARTERS THAT I DROVE

The Turlock Senior Citizens always requested me to drive their Charters. They would take two or three trips to Lake Tahoe or Reno each year, along with a major trip somewhere. They were a fun group to be with and I tried to make each and every trip an enjoyable one for them. They were always a happy bunch going to the Lake but very quiet coming home. I suspect a little loss of money was the reason for this sudden loss of energy.

The Merced Senior Citizens were another group that requested me to drive their Charters. They also made several trips each year to Reno or Lake Tahoe. These trips were mostly to get people out for the weekend in a supervised group. These people would stay home otherwise and never think of driving their cars that far. I was always happy to see the older people make the effort to get out and take these trips. It seemed there were more elderly people in this group also.

On arrival at the Clubs, each passenger was given five or ten dollars in cash plus a free meal ticket, so I am sure some people went along just for the free trip and did no gambling at all. I can't blame them, as this would be a cheap mini-vacation as their rooms were practically free. It was always an overnighter for these groups and they enjoyed going on them, immensely

I would catch lots of Charters when I worked the extra board. Some would be going to baseball games, football games or to San Francisco on a shopping spree. Sometimes it would be a school class going on a field trip.

***

I remember one school trip where I picked up a load of second and third graders from Hughson, California. This is a small rural town southeast of Modesto. I took them to Stanford University to see the newly installed linear accelerator. The children had a fun day and when they went to school the next day, the teacher had each child write a letter, thanking me for the trip.

A couple of weeks later I went to work and the Dispatcher said, "Morgan, you have a bunch of fan mail here." I could not imagine from whom I would be getting mail. I opened a large manila envelope and there were the letters the teacher had the kids write. I will never forget one, written by a boy.

It said, "Dear Mr. Morgan, I sure enjoyed the trip on your bus yesterday. If I had not gone to Stanford with you, I would not have known what a linear accelerator was." I thought to myself, "Son, you must have gotten a lot more out of that trip than I did, because I still don't know what a linear accelerator is!"

***

Charters were an enjoyable part of my work. I have gone to the Opera House in San Francisco and to the Ice Follies. It was always a new and exciting experience on each charter.

Being a Greyhound Driver had its merits. I would almost, and I repeat, almost, drive the buses free of charge to be able to have some of the adventures I had during my career with Greyhound. I feel very lucky to have had all the wonderful experiences that I did during my driving years. I have traveled through out the eleven western states and have been very fortunate in seeing all the National Parks and places of interest. Most of the time all my expenses were paid and this always made the trip more enjoyable.

Everyone always made me feel like part of their big family and showed their appreciation for every thing I did for them that was above and beyond the call of duty. To me it was all a part of my job and I loved to make people happy.

Any time you can look forward to going to work every day, then you are probably doing the thing that you can excel in. I don't think I could have ever chosen a career that would have been more exciting than reporting to work each day, as a Greyhound Bus Driver.

***

I am also an amateur radio operator (K6OEY). One night while talking to some fellow on the radio, he mentioned that he was a teacher at the University of the Pacific and he was taking his Geology Class on a field trip in a couple of weeks. I asked him how his class would be traveling and he said they had chartered a Greyhound Bus for the trip. Until this time I had not told him what I did for a living so I thought this was the time to speak up. I said, "I drive for Greyhound and its too bad I didn't meet you sooner then you could have requested me to drive for your trip." He asked if it was too late to do it now and I told him I didn't know but he would have to write a letter requesting me no later than the next day and take it to the Stockton Dispatcher.

He delivered the letter to the Dispatcher the next day and when I was called to work I was notified I had a request charter. This is the only charter that I actually solicited.

We toured the northern part of California the first couple of days and then we headed south and eventually ended up in San Diego. We stopped at lots of geological spots along the way and I learned what an alluvial fan was. We headed east toward the Salton Sea before starting our trip back to Stockton. By the end of the trip I had a fair knowledge of how this earth was formed. I was told if I took the test that would follow next week, and if I passed it, he would give me points for that semester. I said, "Thanks, but no thanks."

***

The high schools around the Stockton area use to charter Greyhound Buses at the end of the school year to take the seniors on a trip somewhere. At the start of my career we used to take lots of buses up to Yosemite National Park for the day. That seemed to be the "in thing" for the seniors to do for their graduation trips.

Later the fad changed and Disneyland started closing its gates to the general public and letting the seniors in at ten P.M. They would spend the rest of the night there. You could see buses along the highway coming from as far away as Oregon bringing their seniors to Disneyland. Greyhound would have a Motel across the street from Disneyland blocked out for the night for their drivers to get fresh so they could start taking the kids back home the next morning. You cannot believe the turmoil in finding your own bus in the huge parking lot. Somehow it seemed we always recovered all our kids and were ready to leave about an hour after the park closed at 6 AM.

In the latter part of my career we lost all that business to the airlines. Seemed the macho thing to do on your graduation night was to fly to Hawaii. My how times have changed!

***

On one charter I picked up a group of ladies from Modesto and took them to San Francisco for an all day Christmas shopping spree. I let them off at the Greyhound Depot at 7th and Market Street, and I was told to pick them up there at four o'clock that afternoon. At the time it was about nine-thirty and I was thinking of how I could spend the day, as I didn't want to shop. Since the Airlines had only been using

137

jets for a few years, I decided to catch one of our local buses and ride out to the airport.

On arrival at the airport, I was wondering if it was possible to bum a ride on one. Since I was feeling good that day I walked into the terminal and the first thing I spotted was the Pacific Southwest Airlines ticket counter. I walked up to a window and asked where I might find the managers office. The agent pointed to a door across the lobby and I thanked him. I walked over to the door and knocked. (I am in my full Greyhound Uniform). A young lady opened the door and asked me in. I felt kind of silly for a moment but I walked over to the Manager's desk and he asked what he could do for me. I told him I had brought a charter down to SF and was free until four P.M. and since I had never flown in a jet airliner, I was wondering if it might be possible to get a pass to go to Los Angeles and back. He said, "Are you ready to go now?" I said, "Yes."

He looked at his watch and said if I hurried there was a plane loading at gate 42 right now. He told his secretary to write me out a pass. She said, "Shall I charge him tax?" "No," was his reply. With that I was told to have a nice trip and I needed no encouragement, after thanking him I hurried out the door for gate 42.

They were just getting ready to close the door when I arrived but I made it. When I was seated we taxied out to the runway and we were off into the wild blue yonder. Once airborne, I realized I was flying space available and I began to wonder if I would be able to get a flight back to S.F. in time to get back to the Greyhound Depot to pick up my group. I decided since there were flights almost hourly to and from LA, that I should catch the first one back to SF.

When we arrive in LA I grabbed a sandwich out of a vending machine and ate it hurriedly. I then went to the ticket counter and gave the girl my pass. She looked at it and said for me to wait as the flight might be full and since I was flying standby, I could not board at this time.

I began to worry now and I said to myself, "Grady, you might have just screwed up, royally." However the passengers had all gone thru the loading gate and the girl at the ticket counter gave me a call and told me I could board at this time.

At this time PSA did not have a jet way or loading tunnel at the LA airport and I had to go down some steps to the ground level and then walk out to the plane and climb stairs to board. As I was going up the steps I noticed the Captain looking out his window at me. He made a gesture with his hands as to say, what's up?

I made the motion with my hands of turning the steering wheel as if to say, "You want me to drive this thing for you?"

He smiled at me and at that very moment I got an idea, a crazy idea. There were three stews at the top of the stairs and one asked if I had lost my bus. I told her I had but I thought it was in SF and I was going up there to look for it.

I said, "Could I go up front with the crew?"

She said that no one was allowed up there, (I knew that already) since I had bluffed my way this far and since I had already made eye contact with the Captain, I said,

"Would you ask him, please?"

She turned and went into the cockpit and came right back out and said,

"He said to come on in."

When she said that, I made a left turn into the cockpit. The Captain looked back at me when I entered and he introduced himself. He said to tie myself in the seat, behind him, as we were getting ready to depart the terminal. He then introduced me to the Co-pilot who gave me a headset so I could listen to what was going on. We started taxiing out to the active runway for our flight back to SF.

Never in my wildest dreams could I believe any airline would let me do what I had just done. I knew full well that no one was allowed up in the cockpit while in flight, but since my luck was running good that day, I thought I might as well try. The Captain put his job on the line in asking me forward and had I not been in uniform, he would never have given me permission to sit up there with him.

I have to say that the flight home was one of the most exciting times of my life. I learned so much that day about the operations of the airlines and how generous some people are if you only ask.

I told the story to lots of drivers and no one would believe me. Then one day I took another Stockton driver, who just happened to be in SF for the day, out to the airport on a Saturday to take him to LA. We entered the PSA Manager's office and the fellow sitting behind the desk was not the same fellow whom I had seen before and he said he was not authorized to give out passes. However he made a few phone calls to no avail so he apologized and said to come back through the week.

This was enough to convince my driver friend that I had been telling the truth about the other trip. When he got back to Stockton, he set the record straight about my flight to LA. We never got the chance to be in SF at the same time after that and since then, PSA has gone out of business.

***

One charter I caught off the extra board still lives in my mind vividly and to this day whenever I drive up in the mountains and pass thru this area I have to chuckle to myself. I was to pick up a load of kids at a camp on the back road (highway 120).

The instructions on the charter paper said to pass the Office and take the next left turn into a road that would take me to the pick up area. I passed the office and took the road on my left. It was very narrow and I started passing thru some large pine trees that just gave me clearance to get through. I had gone down this road perhaps a hundred yards when a fellow came running and shouting across the little creek on my left.

I stopped and he said that I was not supposed to be in this area. I was to pick up the kids up by the office. I showed him my charter papers and he said he could not imagine who said to do that. I agreed with him. I tried backing up the road I had just come in on but I was unable to get through the large pine trees. He said that I might be able to continue a little further along and turn around in a parking area but it was up a pretty steep hill. When I got to the place I could see there was no way I could get up this hill. I got out of the bus and walked down the road, as I did not want to get the bus any deeper into this situation.

Around the corner was a small concrete bridge crossing the little creek. It was strong enough to support the bus but it was narrow and the turn onto the bridge was too sharp so we started putting rocks in on the left side along the bank to give me a little more room to get onto the bridge.

I decided we had piled enough rocks so I told the fellow to watch my right front wheel to make sure I kept it on the bridge. I got in the bus and started across. The front bumper started to drag but I managed to get the front of the bus onto the bridge. When the left rear wheel got onto the rocks the rear bumper hung up on the roadway. I gunned the engine and the left wheel spun, throwing a rock up into the radiator and steam boiled out the rear of the bus.

That put the icing on the cake and I had to call Stockton and they sent me another bus. Actually they sent two buses, as one was to be used to take the two drivers back to Stockton.

Sometimes you just can't win. I loaded the kids and baggage up by the office and was running about three hours late but I finally got the kids home safely.

I found out later that our large diesel tow truck in SF was sent up to recover the bus. The truck went down the road that I was trying to get to across the creek, and tied a block and tackle to a tree, up the bank across from the bus, and dragged it across the bridge, He attached the cable to the front of the bus and skidded it around parallel to the roadway before they could drive it out. Then the radiator was replaced.

There again, two drivers had to be sent out of Stockton to bring the bus back. That was a very expensive operation created by someone that was careless in giving instructions. I never heard a word from the company about this incident but I wrote a letter, when I got home, explaining what had happened and why it had happened.

These summer charters were taking kids to camps that were in places almost impossible to maneuver a big bus, but somehow we usually made it. I suppose the company took this into consideration when they read these reports. I was determined to never take my bus off the pavement again if I had been given an infraction for this effort.

Chapter 12

THE INSIDE STORY ABOUT GREYHOUND DRIVERS

Any driver that was on a regular run and drove the same schedule every day, at the same time, should have had his rest and would be considered safe to ride with. The drivers working the extra board would be the ones driving the second and third sections of a schedule, and might not have had the proper rest to be considered safe in driving a bus.

I remember the first few years of my driving career. We had Mexican Nationals coming into the area for the tomato harvest. At the end of the tomato harvest we usually had four or five buses at the Stockton Fairgrounds every afternoon at five o'clock, to load up the Mexicans and take them back to Mexico. At that time there was no Interstate highway and highway 99 was a two-lane road going thru every little town between Stockton and Los Angeles. It would take us until after sun up the next morning to get to Indio. We could only drive as far as Indio, California. Our ten hours driving time would be used up and we would be put to bed. By law we could only drive ten hours and then another driver would take the bus on to the border at Mexicali. The other driver would then bring the bus back to Indio where it would be fueled and waiting for us as soon as our eight hours was up. We would then be awakened after six and a half hours (they gave us an hour and a half call) to drive the buses back to Stockton and repeat this trip again and again. As soon as we arrived in Stockton, we would be given eight hours off. Any one knows that you cannot go directly home and to sleep, without spending some time with your family, and maybe have a bite to eat.

The dispatcher will call you one and a half hours before your eight hours are up to report for duty again. After a week of this, especially if you keep catching one of these Mexican moves, you are dead tired. Thank God this only lasted about three weeks to a month.

I can remember, toward the end of the season I was on one of these trips. About thirty miles after leaving San Bernardino, the road was all down hill into Indio. I would be so tired and sleepy by this time, all I could think of was getting into that air-conditioned motel room and to bed.

In those days we were using the old silver side buses that Greyhound had designed, and built for themselves, back in the thirties. These buses are fine while rolling down the highway, but were a bitch to handle in town. They had no power steering and it took two good men and a boy to make a turn into the depot or just make a turn onto any street.

The speedometer on these buses only registered up to eighty miles an hour and then it would start around again. I have seen it pass eighty and register back up to ten on a few trips that I have made going into Indio. That was stupid on my part but that is what happens when one becomes so tired. All the drivers did this when transporting the Mexicans back to the border and it was a very unsafe practice.

All of my driving career, I have said that Greyhound drivers are safe, but we could not take all that credit. God was driving with us when we needed His help. In all the years we transported the Mexicans back to the border, we never had an accident. I know all the drivers were just as tired as I was but we somehow made it safely. Today, when a group of the Stockton drivers get together, someone will mention the Mexican moves we use to have and everyone just laughs and shakes their head in disbelief that we got through those years with no accidents.

We were required by law to have eight hours off between breaks in service. This is eight hours from the time you come in from a tour of duty until you are back in the seat for another tour. You cannot get the rest you need in that amount of time. When you are that tired, you are not as sharp as you should be and your reflexes are not up to par. Most of the time, however, we were not that busy and we could get the proper rest. Through the summer it seemed every schedule would overload and that kept us working short-handed all summer. We always had twenty five to thirty five men working the extra board in Stockton but that was simply not enough at times.

Some times I would look at the names ahead of me on the board, then ask the dispatcher how many known moves he had for the day, and I could come up with a pretty accurate guess as to when I would work again. I could even go fishing sometimes and then come home and get plenty of rest. Some times I would misjudged and would have to go sooner that I expected, then I would be tired. Sometimes we would luck out and go somewhere that we could grab thirty minutes sleep and be refreshed before having to drive again.

I know that God has helped me go through many nights when I should have been home sleeping and not driving a bus with human lives in my hands. When I felt myself getting very tired and knowing I had a long way to go before I could get rest, I would ask God for His help in completing my trip. He has told me many times to relax and stay calm because He is always there riding jump seat and will help me through my trip. I truly believe this to be true.

I remember six months after my first wife and I split up, I was taking the Lodi Travel Club on a trip through the Canyon Lands in Utah. We had left Cedar City, Utah and gone east over the mountain, on our way to Zion National Park. I had not been sleeping well since my divorce because

145

I was still in love with her. I never wanted a divorce. I was very tired from loss of sleep and in going down the mountain on the east side I must have dozed off. When I came to my senses I knew I was speeding and I looked at the speedometer, it was reading seventy-five. Going that fast down hill in a heavy vehicle is an open invitation for trouble. I immediately started applying my brakes but could feel them fading fast. I called on God once more, and asked for His help. Around the next corner the road flattened out long enough to get the bus slowed to a safe speed and shift into a lower gear.

That night, I knelt at the side of my bed and thanked God for his help that afternoon and asked for His help now, to get me over my emotional feeling for my ex-wife. Sooner or later I was going to create an accident and kill a lot of innocent people.

The next morning when I awakened, I found I no longer had feelings for my ex-wife and from that day on she was out of my thoughts completely. I felt a very heavy weight had been removed from my shoulders and I could live again.

Was that help from God? Definitely.

I know that God was riding with me many times during my career with Greyhound and to this day I can feel His presence and only have to ask for His help when the need arises.

I know I am not the only one to be deprived of sleep and on the road when I should not be, because I have talked with, and heard other drivers relate their experiences about fighting sleep. My only answer is --- God has been busy helping them also.

I am often asked by friends and people, how we got by with speeding all the time. Do we have a thing with the California Highway Patrol? My answer is this:

We had governors on all the buses and they are set for the same RPM. This gives us a controlled speed of 62 to 68 miles per hour, depending on the tires on the rear wheels. If the tires are new with lots of tread, then the speed will be higher. If the tires are worn, then the speed will be lower. I drove a different bus every day and I never found a bus with the governor not working properly.

Everyone thinks I am lying when I say that no Greyhound bus could speed. In the twenty- eight years I drove, I had a different bus each day and the governor was working properly on every one of them. People tell me they have been passed by buses going eighty or faster. They just know we speed.

I always ask, "Were you going down hill?"

Some of our drivers would let their schedule buses roll, going down hill, but that is a very bad practice because you can never know what lies ahead, just around the next corner. I even did it going into Indio on the Mexican moves. The brakes are only good for maybe just one emergency stop and if you have been using them too heavily and they are hot, then you will not have any.

On a flat road there is no way a Greyhound bus can go any faster than seventy. When a Greyhound bus passes you, you feel a little push to the right of the road and with the noise from the bus you get the feeling it is going much faster than you.

We had a schedule coming through Stockton at nine fifteen at night and it would be going non-stop to Los Angeles. Lots of times the dispatcher would call me for protection for that schedule (in case of overload) and if I had not gotten plenty of rest that day, I would ask to be dropped. I would then be placed off the board for twelve hours and then placed back on the bottom of the board.

I lost a days pay every time I dropped, but it is hard enough to drive 350 miles to Los Angeles at night, even when fully rested. I felt I would be endangering my life and my passengers if I accepted the assignment. Sometimes there would be three or four drivers in a row dropping that assignment, and the dispatcher had trouble getting someone to come in.

Most of the time all drivers tried to make sure they got their rest because they would suffer if they didn't. In most of our work we would find time to take naps during our layover period. If we went to Lake Tahoe or Reno we could plan on three or four hours sleep while there.

My main concern while operating the buses, were the brakes. Very seldom did I get a bus with good brakes. I learned to drive by staying way ahead of my next move and anticipating the use of the brakes.

I was asked by the dispatcher in Modesto to take a bus back to Stockton. This bus had been parked and left at the depot by a driver on a regular schedule. He had refused to drive it any further. I immediately found out why. The foot brake was useless and I had to use the emergency brake by pulling back on the brake handle in order to stop. I should never have accepted that assignment but I did because the bus was empty and I had plenty of time. I turned on my emergency flashers and drove 25 miles an hour during the thirty miles to Stockton.

If we had a flat or blow out on the highway, we had to change the tire ourselves. The tire weighed in the neighborhood of a hundred pounds or more and they always seemed to blow in the heat of summer. It would take the better part of an hour to get it changed and our uniforms would be filthy. The company would pay for cleaning our uniform and if you tore or damaged it they would buy another one for you. We were only paid six dollars for changing the tire, BIG DEAL.

When the company started hiring women drivers, they could not lift the spare tire so they were allowed to call a tire shop. Naturally that went for the male drivers also. Thank God for women drivers.

There was a lot of jealousy among the drivers working the extra board. Some thought the dispatcher was playing favorites in giving out assignments. I personally know it was done. All the dispatcher had to do was send the first up man on some road test and fifteen minutes later one of his favorites would get a good assignment. The man that went on the road test would return and get some crappy assignment. Some drivers would loan money to certain dispatchers and they would be rewarded handsomely with good moves. Some of the drivers did not like me because they thought I was out soliciting groups to request me to drive their charters for them. All I had to do to keep getting requests was to give the people the service and courtesy they deserved. This was part of my job and I stood out above the rest.

I always made every effort to shift the gears smoothly without jerking heads around. Also I made all my lane changes, while going down the highway, so smoothly that no one noticed I had changed lanes. It took so little effort to be a smooth operator but some drivers did not care. They never once thought about the passengers riding behind them. There is nothing more annoying than trying to sleep on a bus while the driver rolls your head back and forth across the seat, by erratically turning the steering wheel. To me it was also annoying for the driver to hit the brakes and then hit the throttle again, constantly throwing your head forward and backward. There was no need for that type of driving. All it took was to have a little pride in your driving. I would not request any one to be my driver if I had ridden with someone that drove like that.

When I took the job with Greyhound I knew immediately I had a job that I could and would excel in. With so little effort I made my moves flow into one single action. I have had men get off my bus and tell me,

"Driver, you operate this bus as if it were part of you."

I knew he had enjoyed and appreciated the effort I had made in providing a smooth ride, and coming from another man, it meant a lot. Compliments like that made me strive even harder to become a smoother operator. It paid off by my getting a lot of charters.

I suppose it was only a job for a lot of drivers, but to me it was a challenge to give a better ride each time I sat down behind the wheel of a Greyhound bus. I always tried to live up to the words on the little nameplate in the front of the bus, it read:

YOUR OPERATOR

GRADY MORGAN

SAFE-RELIABLE-COURTEOUS

Chapter 13

THE DAY OF THE BIG STRIKE

I had been giving retirement a lot of thought the last few years and had made up my mind to retire at age sixty-two. I had just turned sixty and physically, I felt like a million dollars. I was in very good health and had a feeling that maybe I should continue until age sixty-five. I loved my job, driving and dealing with people so much that I was already beginning to feel sad about leaving all this behind. Many times when I thought about retiring, I would be filled with mixed emotions. Part of me wanted to continue forever and part of me wanted to retire early. Just thinking about retiring brought sadness and an empty feeling to me. I remember thinking, gosh, I hope I don't cry when I step out of the bus for the last time.

Usually when a driver retired, the company would have a photographer or the local newspaper waiting to take his picture, when he stepped out of the bus for the last time. This had been going through my mind for quite some time. I was still two years away from retiring but I had been thinking about it and preparing for it now. I also wanted to take the steering wheel off the last bus I drove as a memento of the many years with Greyhound.

Well, not to worry about my reactions when I turned sixty-two as to whether I would cry or not. I would never have the opportunity to find out. When I came into the Stockton depot from San Francisco the first of October 1983, I stepped out of the bus and the Union steward greeted me with:

"Grady, this is it for a while, we are on strike."

We were on strike for the better part of two months and in the course of that time five of us were fired. There were three drivers and two baggage men fired in the Stockton area.

The company put up a high chain link fence around the property and of course, we were no longer allowed on the property. The Union assigned picket duty to all the members and I was to be there every other day. There were about six to eight union members on the picket line every day. Greyhound hired scab drivers and even some of our own union drivers continued to work. There were a few schedules coming through Stockton but very few passengers were on them.

We had a union rally in Sacramento and we were told not to let the buses into or out of the depots. You don't need to worry about getting fired because we would all go back to work together or none of us would. All we could do in that respect was to stand in the driveway but the police were called and we were told we could not block the driveway. We could, however, as long as we did not stop, walk slowly back and forth across the driveway.

On strike in 1983

152

The driver would slowly keep pushing ahead until he was onto the street again. The secretary to the Stockton superintendent continued working and each day when she finished her shift, the superintendent would drive her home. As they came through the driveway, on the days I was on picket duty, I knelt and looked through the car window, giving her the middle finger. I was one of the five in Stockton that got fired and I know it was because of the action I took against the secretary. The charges against me however, were for Criminal Misconduct. There were never any police called on any of us except for blocking the driveway that one time and there was no damage to any of the buses or property of Greyhound. I think I was fired to set an example for all the younger drivers to let them know that Greyhound would not hesitate to fire any driver, regardless of how long they had been with the company.

During the strike a few of our drivers crossed the picket line and continued working. I must say there were very few of them that did this, though.

We held numerous union meetings during the strike. At one of the meetings, a baggage man from Modesto said his daughter worked in the Modesto City Hospital and had told him there was an urgent need for Mother's milk in the neonatal unit. The Hospital had been receiving Mother's milk from the Santa Clara Valley Medical Center in San Jose by Greyhound. Now that the buses weren't running, they had been unable to obtain the necessary milk without paying a high price to a private company. I volunteered to fly over to San Jose and pick up the milk and deliver it to Modesto. Arrangements were made for members of our union in San Jose to pick up the milk from the medical center and bring it to the San Jose airport. I took the milk and delivered it to Modesto, where H. P. "Hoot" Hildreth, the baggage man, was waiting. Hoot then delivered the milk to the hospital.

On Wednesday December 7, 1983, the Modesto Bee published a story in their paper and I quote:

Strikers made a special milk run

By NANCY NEHER

Bee staff writer

Striking Greyhound bus workers are putting their spare time to good use delivering breast milk for premature babies at Modesto City Hospital.

H.P. "Hoot" Hildreth, An express agent at the Modesto bus terminal, made the first milk run Tuesday, picking up almost a half gallon of it at the Modesto Airport.

The milk, protected in a Styrofoam container, was flown from Santa Clara Valley Medical Center in San Jose to Modesto by a striking Greyhound bus driver, Grady Morgan of Stockton.

"We heard the hospital needed milk so we decided to help," said Hildreth, who dressed in his blue Greyhound uniform to make the run.

Members of the Amalgamated Transit Union Local 1225 donated money to help pay for the plane's fuel to make the run, Hildreth said.

A union steward brought the milk from the San Jose hospital to Morgan's plane at the airport there.

Before the strike, the milk had been delivered by Greyhound bus. Since workers walked off the job more than a month ago and the bus line's schedules were shortened, the hospital has had to find other ways of transporting it.

Until the Greyhound workers volunteered their help, the hospital had to hire a private firm to deliver the milk.

The breast milk is donated by women throughout Northern California and sent to the San Jose medical center where it is tested for bacteria and sterilized, said Susan Vrh, City Hospital spokeswoman.

The milk will keep in a freezer for two weeks.

The breast milk then is distributed where it is needed, Vrh said.

Right now, City Hospital has one infant who needs the donated milk. He is a one and a half month –old boy born prematurely, Vrh said. The infant, who weighs 2 pounds, 9 ounces, needs 5 to 6 ounces of milk a day, she said.

Often there are more infants in the hospital's intensive care nursery who need the breast milk, Vrh said.

Mother's milk is important for premature babies because it is easier to digest and does not cause the allergic reactions that formula often does, Vrh said.

But sometimes a mother is not able to produce any or enough milk for the ailing baby. That's when the hospital asks the milk bank for help, she said.

End of quote.

By Debbie Noda, Bee staff photographer

H.P. Hildreth, right, picks up airlifted milk from
Grady Morgan at the Modesto Airport

When the strike was over everyone went back to work except the five that were fired. The Stockton Record newspaper contacted Greyhound in Phoenix, and asked if the five men that were fired, were going to be put back to work. The Record published an article in the paper saying Greyhound considered us dangerous to the public and we would never work again for Greyhound.

We filed a class action suit against Greyhound for that statement and we were awarded twenty five thousand dollars.

I explained in other parts of this book, that I finally negotiated my own settlement with Greyhound, to get my record cleared and to go back to work. It was then I followed through with my request for my retirement, and I never got to find out, --- if I would have really cried on my final day of work.

The Union kept negotiating with the representative in Phoenix, that was handling my case, but it seemed they were getting nowhere. It had been about seven months since the strike had been settled and the chances of my returning to work looked bleak.

One Friday morning, I decided to call Phoenix, and I asked for the person in charge of the negotiation with the Union concerning my case. When he came on the line, I introduced myself and said I would like to talk to him about my case. He immediately said, "Grady you know we can't discuss this issue."

"I realize that," I replied. "But you and I are both grown men and if we can settle this issue, one on one, then I will write a letter to the Union and submit my request through the proper channels.

After a long hesitation he said, "I don't see why we can't do that. Grady, tell me exactly what you expect and what it would take to please you in settling this case." he continued.

I said, "All I want is to have my record cleared, and I think I deserve the wages I have lost since the strike was settled, that is all." He asked what run I was on and in a couple minutes he came up with a figure. He said he saw no reason to keep this case open any longer. I was told he was coming to San Francisco the following Tuesday and for me to have a letter in the Union office and he would authorize it and my case would be closed.

In a couple weeks I received the largest pay check I could every have dreamed of. When I received the check of seven months back pay, all in one check, it was almost more than my wife could handle.

I can truthfully say that I do not think I could have ever found a career that suited me more and one that I was so happy with. The last few years of my operating schedules, I was dealing with pot smokers every day and that did tarnish the job some, but even with that distraction, I still loved my work.

As far as the Amalgamated Transit Union is concerned, the Union President lied to me during the Sacramento rally when he said, during the strike, "Do not worry about getting fired fellows, because we will all go back to work together or no one will."

All it would have taken at that time was for the Union to tell Greyhound the same thing they told us and we would all have gone back together. Instead everyone trampled over us in getting the buses rolling again without one thought about our welfare.

Am I still a supporter of the Amalgamated Transit Union, after having to negotiate my own return to work?

Draw your own conclusion.

There was no damage done to any bus or Greyhound property. Yes, there were lots of ugly words said, but that is a common thing in all strikes. When a strike is over, all is forgotten, and the company and employees become one big happy family again.

In previous strikes, after they were settled, I remember sitting and drinking coffee with the supervisor and dispatchers and we would laugh about what went on during the strike.

I simply could not think of leaving a company that had treated me so well, and one that I loved so much, without first getting my record clean. Now that all this is behind me, I feel good about the company and after being retired for twenty years, I am enjoying my retirement to the fullest.

***

The life of a Greyhound driver is, was, or has been a very exciting one, but now I feel I should-------------

LEAVE THE DRIVING TO SOMEONE ELSE!

Chapter 14

MY LIFE AFTER GREYHOUND

When I was fired from Greyhound during the strike of 1983, and finally got my record cleared of all infractions, I retired with a feeling that I had fulfilled a dream in my career, doing what I enjoyed most. Now it was time for me to move forward to another stage of my life in which I am supposed to enjoy the good life, kick back and enjoy what is left.

My wife, Linda, and I had just built a new home in Stockton and were very happy there. She was a travel agent and we had the opportunity for a lot of free travel, or at a greatly reduced price, so we took advantage of it.

We went to New Zealand for two weeks and visited both, the North and South Island. This was a very interesting trip but we could not get over the fact there were no fast food places along the road as we traveled throughout the countryside. We went for long stretches without food sometimes simply for the lack of a place to eat. Then when we did find a café, we had a choice of boiled, fried or roasted mutton, which neither of us could eat. There were a few, "take away's," which was the equivalent of our drive-through. You could get some funny looking french-fries and some sort of mutton sandwich to eat there or take out. Or else take some sort of mutton sandwich and some funny looking french-fries. Either way you would be eating mutton of some sort.

Over all, the trip was beautiful and we spent lots of time parked in the green countryside, watching little lambs, playing together like school children. There was lots of snow on the mountains and the rivers were spectacular. This country is supposed to have the best trout fishing of any place in the world. We used most of our two-week package just driving from Auckland to the southern most part of South Island. We spent the night in Wellington and the next morning we turned in our rental car and boarded the ferry that took us across the channel to Nelson. Another rental car was waiting for us when we got off the ferry and we continued our way south. There was lots of beauty to be seen everywhere. It was the start of spring down there and it was late summer when we left home.

We were given a little book in our travel package that had four or five motels listed in each town, along the way, and we could have our choice of where we stayed each night. We usually chose the first one we came across as they were all equal in value and we found them all to be very clean. There was always a half pint of cream in each little refrigerator to be used in our tea since all the locals drank tea.

One thing that I noticed, besides driving on the wrong side of the road, was the fact while on South Island, all the bridges were one lane. It seemed odd to me at the time but after I got home, it occurred to me that there was no need for two lane bridges. I never met or saw a car at any time while crossing a bridge. The population on South Island is very small compared to that on North Island, yet South Island is twice the size. There are more sheep than people.

We stopped at a beautiful lake and watched some black swans swimming near the road. The country was full of things to see and lots of things that we do not have at home. They raise red deer on ranches for commercial use. The red deer were larger than the deer we have here. I suppose they would be about the size of the mule deer in our country. At one point on South Island, there was a glacier that extended all the way down to within a half mile of the ocean. We drove as close to the glacier as we could and then walked out on it. It wasn't really that cold there and it is surprising to believe the glacier was that close to the ocean.

We spent the night in Christchurch and visited a beautiful museum of the Maori's, depicting the native culture of the Island. There was also volcanic action in the area with lots of bubbling mud pots with steam escaping everywhere.

From Christchurch we crossed the mountains and drove down the west side of South Island. Our final destination was Milton Sound where we spent our last two days.

The day before we were supposed to fly home, we were still on the very extreme southern end of South Island. We had planned it that way, as we would be taking a plane back into Auckland. We would have to back track over territory we had already driven since there was only one road running the length of South Island.

New Zealand is a beautiful place to visit and I highly recommend it. It did not take too long to get adjusted to driving on the left side of the road. The first afternoon we were there, our rental car was delivered to us and we decided we should venture out into some traffic and try our luck. I had never driven a car with the steering located on the right side, nor had I ever driven on the left side of the road. We had a city map of Auckland and we were not too far from the harbor so we decided to take a drive down there. Our rental car was a Toyota and of all things it had to be a stick shift. Now I have no trouble driving a stick shift but everything is located on the right side of the car and it was hard getting use to the throttle being against the right wall.

We left the motel and I signaled for a right turn at the first corner but the windshield wipers came on instead. We had our first laugh at my driving. I got moving again and I thought I was doing very well, as I was staying on the extreme left side of the street, minding my own business. There was a policeman parked at the curb and when I passed him, he immediately pulled out behind me with red lights flashing and my first impulse was to get to the right side of the road but I remembered where I was so I stopped in my lane and the officer pulled up on my right side. He asked where we were from and how long we had been in Auckland.

I said, "We are from California and we have been here for about an hour."

He said, "I thought so. Here in New Zealand you are required to wear seat belts at all times, so buckle up and enjoy your visit."

What a nice reception and relief to find I was not into as much trouble as I thought. It was a breeze from there on except for their roundabouts. I never became comfortable with them all the time I was there. Lucky for me, I only found them in Auckland.

With all these new experiences behind us, with loads of pictures, it was time to board the plane for the long fifteen-hour flight back home. Being a pilot and having a love for flying, I can truthfully say this is one time I got tired of flying.

***

I was reading the newspaper one Sunday morning after we had returned from New Zealand and saw an advertisement in the travel section on the Great Wall of China. I have always wanted to see and walk on The Great Wall, and the price was right, so we booked an eleven-day trip to China.

At this time, Linda was about two years into her struggle with breast cancer and I was worried about her making the trip but she did enjoy going to China and had no problems. Her Doctor said it would be good for her to go.

We flew out of San Francisco on Air China. We were aboard a Boeing 747 and when we left San Francisco we were never out of sight of land very long, as we went up the west coast to Anchorage and across the Aleutian Islands. We crossed the Bering Straits, the Kamchatka Peninsula, across the Sea of Okhotsk and into Manchuria. From there we entered China just north of Beijing. Beijing is a city with well over twelve and a half million people. It is a modern city with tall buildings comparable to our large cities. In fact if it were not for the people you might think you were in San Francisco or Los Angeles. There were little red cabs, (three passenger), running by the hundreds, all over the city. The driver is in the only seat in front and he is enclosed in a protective cage. For what reason I did not know.

Streets in Beijing—little red cars are taxis

The English language is compulsory in their schools there and I had no trouble finding someone to answer my questions in English. We took a ride in a rickshaw for about three blocks, being pulled by a man on a bicycle. He darted out across the street without looking back at the traffic, and I knew I would never be able to write this story but by a miracle, we were not hit. When I got out of the rickshaw I wanted to get a picture of Linda sitting there. I paid for our ride (one dollar) and then motioned for the driver to stand by Linda so I could get a picture of him also.

He did so and then said, "Three dolla."

The picture cost more than the ride.

The second day we took a tour to the Tiananmen Square. This is the largest public square in the world. In the summer of 1989 there was an uprising of college kids and protestors in this square and the Red soldiers ran over some with tanks and shot others. The Chinese government warned the hospitals not to treat any of the wounded or there would be severe repercussions. Our tour guide did not want to say anything about the incident. All he would say was that he didn't remember. Tiananmen Square is about four city blocks pushed together. It is a huge place and is covered with rough bricks. There are two hundred or so people there at all times. You will see at least a half dozen red Chinese soldiers patrolling in pairs as you walk across the square.

Tiananmen Square---This area is about four blocks square

164

We continued across the Square and through the Forbidden City and the Imperial Palace that day. It took most of the day just peeking into all the rooms.

The next day we boarded an Air China Bus and it took us about thirty-five miles north of Beijing, to see the Great Wall. The Great Wall starts at the Yellow Sea and runs about 3500 miles across the northern border of China. It is built mostly through mountainous terrain and usually follows the ridges. It runs through some of the most barren and impassible country. I was simply amazed at the huge stones that were used in building the wall. At the time it was being built, there was no way to get any equipment into the area. This work was done by cheap Chinese labor, and should one of the workers die while working, he was buried in the wall and they moved on.

Portion of the Great Wall

There are guardhouses built on the wall in order to shoot anyone caught trying to climb over the wall with ladders. These guardhouses were manned and were spaced so there was no unprotected area. The wall is about twenty feet high and without a ladder of some sort, one would be hard pressed to climb it.

I only walked up one section of the Wall as far as the first guardhouse. It gets very steep in some areas and then you have steps to contend with that are at different heights. It was interesting to see how the Wall was constructed and I am glad to have had the opportunity to see and walk on it. We visited several points of interest on our way back to our hotel making for a full day of sight seeing.

I found there was lots of fine dust in the air that was caused by storms up in Manchuria. These are storms originating quite often from the Kobe dessert and dust drifts down and settles across northern China.

The Air China bus we used for tours

We left Beijing and flew to Xian (pronounced, "she-aun"), which is about two hundred miles west of Beijing. A farmer just out side of town had started digging a well and had unearthed a terra cotta soldier. On further investigation he found another and then another. It soon became a monumental historical find and the authorities then came in and started uncovering more soldiers and their horses. It is very odd that no two of these soldiers are alike. Each of them had their hands cupped as if holding a spear or heavy weapon. Of course the wood had long since rotted away.

The area is now enclosed in a building the size of a football field. No picture taking is allowed inside the building except one area where I was able to take these pictures. There are guards posted all along the perimeter of the building to see that the orders are followed. The Tara Cotta soldiers were definitely a worthwhile visit. When we were there they were still unearthing more soldiers.

Some of the Tara Cotta soldiers and horses

These soldiers were facing away from the tomb of the king they were supposed to be protecting and they were supposed to look like an army watching over the tomb, frightening away any intruders. Each of these figures was different and I can only imagine the difficulty involved in making them.

When we arrived in China, I noticed many Red Soldiers in uniform and they seemed to be everywhere we went.

The streets of Beijing would be a terrible place to learn how to drive. No one gives the right of way to anyone and to step off the curb against a green light is almost a guarantee of losing a part of your body. However, we never saw any accidents while we were there. I learned very quickly, pedestrians do not have the right of way in China. A bicycle even clipped me once while trying to cross the street on a green light. The driver of our tour bus would pull out over a double yellow line to pass someone and the car coming toward us had better move over because we were coming through. I was always very cautious when I crossed the street, even when I had a green light.

Our tour bus was built in China and was very modern and comfortable. I think the Chinese government sponsored the complete tour by providing 747's, our hotels, and the bus. We used Air China to fly both to and from the west coast. I was very satisfied with all the services and it seemed like they were feeding us every couple of hours. The soft drink bar was open at all times and you were welcome to just help yourself to whatever you wanted. It was a sixteen-hour trip going over and thirteen hours coming home.

We left Xian and flew down to Shanghai for two days. I was not really impressed with that area. We went on several tours of the city and once again we saw lots of people. I could easily understand the need for population control. The day for us to return home came too quickly, but it was time to go.

We flew a new 767 from Beijing to Xian and a new 777 from Xian to Shanghai. We boarded an Air China 747 in

Shanghai, and we were soon on our way home. We flew north to Tokyo and made a right turn, heading straight to San Francisco with the jet stream.

The Air China 747 has a huge map showing the coastline of the Western USA, including the Pacific Ocean and Eastern Asia. There was a little plane (representing ours) flying the course we were taking and it kept us updated as to where we were at all times. There was also an airspeed indicator that gave us our true ground speed. I would not have believed it had I not seen it, but at one time while crossing the pacific, it was showing 767 miles per hour. The jet stream was really giving us a push.

***

After coming home from some of the Canadian trips that I took I had told Linda about the beauty of the Canadian Rockies and I wanted to follow through with my promise to take her there. After a couple months rest we left for Canada. We followed highway 97 up through Kelowna into Revelstoke. She was not feeling too good at this time so I did not want to take too long in getting there. The main points of interest were going to be the Rogers Pass, Lake Louise, Columbia Ice Fields, Jasper, Banff, Calgary and down to Glacier National Park in Montana.

Rogers pass is my favorite spot along the Trans-Canada Highway. You are at the summit of the Rockies and snow covers the mountains all around you regardless of the time of year. It is such a spectacular view and gives you a preview of things to come.

We arrived at Lake Louise late in the evening so we spent the night at the foot of the hill instead of going directly to Lake Louise. The next morning there was an inch of snow on top of my car. We visited Lake Louise and then continued on to the Columbia Ice Fields. We walked a short way out onto the Glacier but quickly returned to the car, as it was very cold. We continued on to Jasper and spent the night there. Linda was not feeling up to much activity so we did not spend too much time in Jasper. We started on our way back to Banff and did some sightseeing when we arrived in Banff.

A quaint little motel before reaching Rogers Pass

We took a tram ride up the mountain behind Banff to see the view.

View from tram

Then we drove out to the golf course and watched the Elk feeding there. At this time Linda was getting tired and we had a long way to go even if we came straight home so we went through Calgary without stopping on the way down to Glacier Montana. We drove through the park and started our trek for home.

Elk resting on golf course

Maligne Lake—near Lake Louise

Top of "Going to the sun" pass in Glacier

I thought after the Canadian trip that Linda would never be up to going any where with me again. She was fighting every day for her life and she did not give up easy. I knew someday soon she could not go any more, and I wanted to do everything I could to make her last days happy. I decided to let her be the judge of when to stop going.

After the trip to Canada we didn't travel for about six months, then Linda surprised me one day by asking if I still wanted to go to Albuquerque to the Hot Air Balloon Fiesta. I told her I would like to and she asked if she could go along.

***

We left the first of October and visited the Grand Canyon, as she had never been there. We drove through the Petrified Forest and the Painted Desert. We continued on to Albuquerque for the Balloon Fiesta.

I had never been to the Hot Air Balloon Fiesta so this would be a first for me. You have to get up early in the morning and be out at their site at the crack of dawn and it just happened to be mighty cold that early in the morning. We stayed two days and watched the "Specialty" balloons, which turned out to be my favorites. There were balloons in the shape of trucks, beer bottles, wedding cakes, animals and anything you might see crawling or flying.

I was amazed at the specialty balloons that were flying. The envelope alone (air bags) cost thousands of dollars. The envelope is only good for five hundred hours of flying before it has to be discarded. Unlike an airplane, it will start depreciating the first hour it is used. At times there were as many as twelve hundred balloons at the Fiesta. That was just to many to handle so they have put a limit on the entries to one thousand balloons.

We enjoyed the morning watching balloons floating across the sky, and at times through the day, they would hover above us since there would be very little wind blowing to move them along.

The Albuquerque Hot Air Balloon Fiesta is a must to see, as it is the largest gathering of hot air balloons in the world.

We went up to Santa Fe, as Linda always talked about and wanted to go to Santa Fe and Taos. Both of these cities are above 7000 feet. They are both located in the high desert country with mountains in the background. Both Cities are in flat country however and you would never believe you were at that elevation.

We spent two days in the Santa Fe-Taos area and then began our trek back toward home.

We went through Utah and visited Bryce and Zion National Parks on our way. We did not spend much time at either Park but at least she got to see them.

Before we got to the California border on highway 120, we came upon a spectacular rock formation and I stopped to take a few pictures. When I came back to the car, Linda had gotten out and was stretched out on a large rock.

She said, "Just leave me here, I'm tired."

The thirtieth anniversary of the hot air balloons

This was the last trip we made together. It was the middle of October 2000, and when we got home, Linda started going down hill very fast. Bear in mind, we were divorced these last few trips but I still felt an obligation to make her life as happy and enjoyable as I possible could. I spent every day with her and took her to all her treatments.

In the middle of December 2001, her son, Darrin, and I started a twenty-four hour vigil with her. On Christmas day, I had finished my day shift with her and was dead tired. When Darrin came, to be with her through the night, I felt the time was near and I would probably never see her alive again. She had been in a coma for the past week and I told Darrin when she expired to call me immediately. I knew she would not make it through the night. At 7:30 P.M. he called.

I went over to see Linda for the final time and said my last good bye and came home.

It was Christmas Day---What a terrible time to go.

***

For the first six months I felt lost and had no desire to do anything. I felt time was passing me by though and I was not through living yet. Being out of the circuit for the past four years, and at my age, I wondered who would have me. Well it seems all things have a happy ending sometimes, and two years later when I met De, who had lost her husband recently, my life changed completely.

De's sister had worked in a restaurant in Lodi where I use to eat quite often. She had recently moved to Georgia but we still communicated by E-mail regularly. In one of her letters she told me about her sister, De, and suggested I write her a letter as we both could use another friend. In fact she said she was going to E-mail her sister and tell her she would be receiving a letter from me.

How easy is that to meet someone? I wrote a letter of introduction to De and got a reply immediately. De had just retired and was in fact coming to Lodi the next week to visit her other sister. The first night De arrived, we went to dinner and we have been together since. We were together constantly for the next six weeks and we wasted no time in making our decision to get married. It was a little soon, as some might think, but for us it was the right time and it has been fantastic. We bought a nice mobile home in Galt, California and hopefully this is where we will finish our lives.

***

I think God watches over us at all times, and when the pressure gets to great, or our load too heavy, He steps in and gives us a little boost. I feel He has come to my aid again, as I now have a happy life that I thought would never be mine.

***

De and I have many trips planned for the years to come and once again we will be sharing the beauty of this great nation.

I once read a poem that has meant so much to me and I quote:

A Happiness shared by one is half a happiness.

A Happiness shared by two is twice a happiness.

A sorrow shared by one is twice a sorrow.

A sorrow shared by two is half a sorrow.

Author unknown

Chapter 15

A PERSONAL PART OF MY LIFE

During my lifetime there have been numerous trials and tribulations. I sometimes wonder why these things happened to me but it has been my belief that God only gives you what you can handle at any one time.

When my first wife and I divorced, it was the start of my life almost coming apart.

It took quite sometime to overcome the hurt I was carrying over our breakup. I never wanted a divorce.

Then Kenneth was killed in 1971, I thought my world would end but through my trust in the Lord, I survived. At that time I had a talk with God and told Him I needed all the help I could get from Him if I were to continue living. Kenneth was my only son and had just reached the prime of his life.

Then over a period of years I lost my youngest daughter to breast cancer. She had almost reached the point of being cured when it struck again, with vengeance. This time it took her life.

I have pictures of my other two children, Sylvia and Kenneth, in some of my stories and I felt it only fair to add this chapter and put Marcia's story and picture in my book.

Marcia was married to Brian Sampson and they had two beautiful boys, Scott and Sean. Scott had just graduated from high school in Temecula, California and Marcia was very proud of her boys.

Brian was very successful in the real estate business and they owned a beautiful home in Temecula. Everything was definitely going their way when Marcia was diagnosed with breast cancer. She underwent chemo treatments and the doctor said the cancer was in remission. The doctor had her taking some medication that was supposed to keep the cancer from ever returning and we thought she had the problem licked.

Marcia had gone to Sacramento to visit one of her friends when she ran short of her medication. She went to the pharmacy chain she had been using in Temecula to have it refilled. On picking up the prescription she noticed the pills were different and on questioning the pharmacist they discovered the pharmacy in Temecula had been giving her an iron pill with almost the same name.

Marcia had been taking the wrong medication for about a year before the mistake was discovered and by that time the cancer had been feeding on the iron pill and come back with vengeance.

Knowing she only had a short time to live, Brian fulfilled one of Marcia's wishes by taking the family and spending a week in Yellowstone National Park. Marcia wanted the family to spend one last vacation together and she had wanted to go to Yellowstone for some time.

She suffered a lot on that trip because one hip was cracked and very painful but she endured the pain.

After returning home, her condition deteriorated rapidly and she passed away the following February.

My youngest daughter, Marcia Lou

Chapter 16

A REFLECTION OF MY LIFE

In this assortment of stories, I have tried to bring to you the parts of my life that I remember best, from early childhood to the present time. I now consider most of my mistakes either way behind me or it is too late to think about making changes now.

***

I can remember when I was five years old, I had been having terrible earaches for sometime and the doctor told my parents that I should have my tonsils removed. The day of the surgery I can remember my dad taking me into the doctor's office and the doctor put a cloth over my face and I was out like a light. When I awakened, my dad was sitting and holding me in the hallway, just outside the doctor's office. After a while the doctor came out into the hall and took a look at my throat and I distinctly remember him saying,

"Sanford, why don't you take this boy and get him an ice cream cone?"

***

I also remember every Saturday the whole family would get in the old Model T and we would be off to town for the day. On Saturday morning my job was to shell a sack full of corn to take to the Mill. We would drop the sack off as we went into town and pick up the corn meal on our way home. The mill took a portion of the corn so there was no charge for the grinding. We would usually get into town around ten o'clock in the morning. The theater opened at eleven and I usually made it in time for the first show. My dad always gave me a quarter to spend and that would get me into the show and buy a bag of popcorn, all for fifteen cents. After the show I would go around into a little alley to "Hap's Hamburger Stand." and buy me a hamburger and co cola with the remaining ten cents and then I would be broke.

***

I remember the times in my early teens when my dad would let me drive the old model T into Forreston, all by myself, to get ice and a loaf of bread for Sunday dinner. We always had ice tea and a loaf of, "store bought bread," with our dinner on Sunday. I had no driver's license and I am not sure that I had to have one at that time.

***

I had lots of growing up to do and when I went to Hawaii at age eighteen, I learned to change the way I talked and started working on losing my Texas accent. I took a lot of kidding about my speech, and I was really self-conscious, so I started eliminating phrases that Texans use. Things like "you all, down yonder, can I carry you to the store and such phrases we used every day in Texas. Most people can't believe I am really a Texan when they hear me talk now.

***

I can remember playing rubber guns with my friends. I was always Gene Autry or one of the good guys wearing a white hat. I remember one day we got tired of playing cowboys and Indians so I thought up another plan for having fun for the four of us. We made ping-pong paddles for each of us and I said follow me. I had found a bumblebee nest in the ground, out in the pasture. I had a short block of wood with a nail driven into it with a long piece of string attached. We

181

found the nest and I put the block of wood over the hole and then we stomped the ground to make the bees angry. Each of us got back about ten yards from the hole and we had the four points of the compass covered when I jerked the block of wood from the hole. The bees popped straight up out of the hole and took a bearing on us and came straight for our faces. We would hit them like batting a ping-pong ball. Everything would be fine until a lucky bee got through to someone, then the "stingee" would run and jump into the creek. That would make us one man short and there would be more bees coming at us until some one else got stung and then there would be only two fighters left and it wasn't long before there was only one left. He might as well give up because he couldn't handle the job by himself. I remember getting stung once and I ran to the creek and jumped in and stayed under water as long as I could and when I came up for air, the bumble bee got me on the forehead before I had gotten the water out of my eyes.

What pain we would endure, just for a good bumblebee fight! Why we actually thought it was fun I will never know. I suppose it was just another way of entertaining ourselves since we had no TV.

***

One day our gang was roaming around and came upon an old abandoned house. We saw a huge wasp nest under the eave of the house. We couldn't find a pole or anything to knock it down but I came up with a brilliant idea. I would climb upon the roof and take a short stick and lean over the eave and I could get it then. Smart idea! When I reached under the eave and knocked the nest down about two hundred mad wasps had me on the roof with out any escape route. I was stung so many times I lost count, but the stings were not the worst part. I jumped off the roof, which was at least fifteen feet high, and fortunately I survived without breaking anything. I remember, after it was over, I thought, now that was a dumb thing to do!

As I got older I began to make better use of my time. My dad had bought a twenty-two rifle for me when I was five years old and I use to go down on the river squirrel hunting with him. We had red squirrels in Texas and they were very good eating. This was during the depression years and meat of any sort was appreciated. I started hunting cottontail rabbits to put on our table in lieu of fried chicken. One of our friends in town asked if I would bring her some rabbits and she would give me ten cents a piece for them. I started my little meat packing company that day by taking her three rabbits, which I sold at a bargain price, three for a quarter. She told her neighbor about the rabbits and by word of mouth the news spread until I was hunting rabbits everyday after school and I sold three every day. For once I didn't have to ask my dad for a nickel or dime any more as I always had change in my pocket.

At the time I could buy a box of fifty twenty-two shells for nine cents at the Western Auto Store and I never wasted my shots so they would last me a long time. I started saving my money and was able to buy my graduation suit on my own. I only paid nineteen dollars for that suit. They were cheap in those days, but not really too cheap as wages were next to nothing then.

***

I think being brought up during the depression days was an asset for me. I learned where and how to make money and to appreciate what I had. We were poor money wise but we were rich just having enough food to eat. We had plenty of eggs, milk, butter, and vegetables were plentiful as we raised a huge garden every year. We never went hungry. We butchered four pigs every winter and ate ham, sausage and bacon all thru the year. I remember the big biscuits with a large slice of ham on it in my lunch box. The city kids would sometimes trade a sandwich with real light bread and some fancy filler for one of my biscuits and ham.

***

I remember going bowling with three of my friends in Honolulu. We were all about nineteen years old and ran around together when we weren't working. Some one suggested we go bowling and I said I had never bowled but we went anyway. It was decided the lowest score would buy dinner for the group. They really thought they had a sucker until the game was over and my score was the second highest. They never did believe that this was the first game I had ever bowled.

***

Today I am living the happy life one should expect in his golden years. My wife and I are happy together, doing the things we both love. We have traveled each year to distant points of interest and as long as our health holds out, we will continue to do so.

***

If I had my life to live over I don't think I would change very much. In the early years when we were short of money, I put a value on that time as a learning experience in handling money later in life. My dad taught me to be honest and he made sure I led a Christian life during my youth. After leaving home I continued living a Christian life. There was a period of time I got out of touch with the church but was never out of touch with God.

***

One thing I would have changed, if it had been possible, was to become an airline pilot instead of a bus driver. At the time, all airlines were flooded with ex-military pilots wanting jobs. They had hundreds of hours of flying time, and

I had accumulated very few. I did not stand a chance of working for the airlines as a pilot.

***

Given a choice, I would have certainly had my two children out live me. That is the way it is supposed to be but in my case, it did not work out.

***

Could I have made more out of myself than what I did? I suppose, but I was happy. I consider the happiness and contentment one achieves in doing, what ever they do while going through life, to be the answer to that question.

***

Yes, I could have possibly made more money and had a larger home and had a more expensive car to drive, but would that have made me happier? No, I was happy with what I had and I think I achieved what I wanted in my life.

I always wanted to own and fly my own airplane. I have owned four airplanes during my life so that dream has been fulfilled. I worked in construction while I was growing up and I had a dream of building my own home someday, with my bare hands. I have built two houses with beautiful fireplaces during my life, so that dream was fulfilled.

Could I have done more?

***

To me, life is all about being the best you can be, not being judged by your riches or how much you have acquired throughout life. I feel I have reached all the goals in my life, meager as they may be, and in getting there I have always had God walking by my side and, thereby, found the happiness and contentment I was seeking.